MINDFIRE

BIG IDEAS FOR CURIOUS MINDS

SCOTT BERKUN

Mindfire: Big Ideas for Curious Minds
By Scott Berkun

ISBN: 978-0-9838731-0-5
Published by: Berkun Media, LLC
Editor: Krista Stevens
Cover Designer: Tim Kordik
Interior Designer: Tim Kordik
Brewmaster: Tim Kordik
Editor and Proofreader: Marlowe Shaeffer

Printing History: October 2011: First Edition
Disclaimer: While no precaution has been spared in the safe preparation of this book, the publisher and author assume no responsibility for errors or omissions, or for damages resulting from driving, knife juggling, or leopard wrangling performed while simultaneously reading this book. The makers of this book also wish to convey our complete lack of accountability if you literally set minds or physical objects on fire without explicit written permission from your mom and the mothers of all those involved.

TABLE OF CONTENTS

GET **READY**

WARNING: THREE IMPORTANT THINGS

Welcome to this book. I'm glad you're here. Before the book begins, there are three things you need to know:

1. These essays have been published elsewhere before. Do not panic.

2. If you are so inclined, you can find them for free by poking around on scottberkun.com or elsewhere online. I recommend you don't do that. Here's why.

If you're new to my work, this book serves as a fantastic introduction to a decade of effort. All the essays have been edited, washed, organized, re-organized, washed again, stared at crossly, then pruned, polished and curated for your pleasure. It's the best possible edition of these works.

If you've previously enjoyed my work online, please pay a few bucks in return for the value my free work has provided. Karma is good for you and for me. You'll enjoy rereading past essays, or ones you missed, in this simple, convenient, beautiful book.

3. This book is self-published. I've had an excellent relationship with O'Reilly Media, the publisher of my first three books. But I know I want to publish books in the future that no publisher in its right mind would release. Therefore, I must learn to do it myself. What you have in your hands is a purely independent production.

There. You've been lovingly warned. Now the preface patiently awaits your attention.

PREFACE:
PLEASE ACTIVATE YOUR MIND

These essays were made to challenge minds. I'll be thrilled if you like what I say, but if you don't, that's fine, provided I get you thinking.

Most days we avoid big thoughts. We stay busy with small things. Despite our wishes, we know real thinking takes us places we may not be prepared for. You may finish this book with questions you wish I'd answered instead of the ones you found. But that list might be more valuable to you than you think.

As a collection of previously published works, written independently, you should feel free to read them in the fashion you choose. They were selected for this book because they fit the theme of intelligent provocation, and ordered, after much experimentation, in a simple and straightforward way. But if you disagree, your vote trumps mine; skip sections, read the essays in reverse order, have a beer after each paragraph, any means you choose is fine with me.

If you find anything you like here, please join me online at **www.scottberkun.com** where the quest for wisdom continues.

Scott Berkun
9/20/2011

PART ONE
GASOLINE

THE CULT OF BUSY

When I was young I thought busy people were more important than everyone else. Otherwise, why would they be so busy? I had busy bosses and busy parents, and I assumed they must have important things to do. It seemed an easy way to decide who mattered and who didn't. The busy must matter more and the lazy mattered less. This is the cult of busy: by always doing something, we assume you must be important or successful.

The cult of busy explains the behavior of many people. By appearing busy, others bother them less, and simultaneously believe they're doing well. It's quite a trick.

I believe the opposite to be true. Or nearly the opposite. Here's why: time is the singular measure of life. It's one of the few things you cannot get more of. Knowing how to spend it well is the most important skill you can have.

The person who gets a job done in one hour seems less busy than the guy who can only do it in five. How busy a person seems is not necessarily indicative of the quality of their results. Someone who is better at something might very well seem less busy, simply because they are more effective. Results matter more than the time spent achieving them.

Being in demand can have good and bad causes. Someone with a line of people waiting to talk to them outside their office door seems busy, and therefore important. But somehow the clerk running the slowest supermarket checkout line in the universe isn't praised in the same way; it means they're ineffective. People who are at the center of everything aren't necessarily good at what they do (although they might be). The bar of being busy falls far below the bar of being good.

The compulsion to save time may lead nowhere. If you're always cutting corners to save time, when exactly are you using all that time you've saved? There is this illusion that, someday, you'll get back all that time you've squirreled away in one big chunk. Time doesn't work this way. For most Americans, our time savings goes into watching television. That's where all the time savings we think we get actually goes.

The phrase "I don't have time for" should never be said. We all get the same amount of time every day. If you can't do something, it's not about the quantity of time. It's really about how important the task is to you. I'm sure that if you were having a heart attack, you'd magically find time to go to the hospital. That time would come from something else you'd planned to do, but now seems less important. This is how time works all the time. What people really mean when they say "I don't have time" is that this particular thing is not important enough to earn their time. It's a polite way to tell people they're not *worthy*.

This means that people who are always busy are time poor. They have a time shortage. They have time debt. They are either trying to do too much, or they aren't doing what they're doing very well. They are failing to be effective with their time, or they don't know what they're trying to effect, so they scramble at trying to optimize for everything, which leads to optimizing nothing.

People who truly have control over time always have some in their pocket to give to someone in need. A sense of priorities drives their use of time and it can shift away from the ordinary work that's easy to justify, in favor of the more ethereal, deeper things that are harder to justify. They protect their time from trivia and idiocy; these people are time rich. They provide themselves with a surplus of time. They might seem to idle, or relax more often than the rest, but that just might be a sign of their mastery, not their incompetence.

I deliberately try not to fill my calendar. I choose not to say yes to everything. Doing so would make me too busy and less effective at achieving my goals. I always want to have some margin of time in reserve, time I'm free to spend in any way I choose, including doing almost nothing at all. I'm free to take detours. I'm open to serendipity. Some of the best thinkers throughout history had some of their best thoughts while going for walks, playing cards with friends—little things that aren't considered the hallmarks of busy people. It's the ability to pause, to reflect, and relax, to let the mind wander, that's perhaps the true sign of time mastery. When a mind returns it is sharper, more efficient, and perhaps most important, calmer than before.

WANTS VS BELIEFS

A funny thing about the human mind is it tends to believe what it wants to believe. We allow what we want to have happen distort our reasoning on how likely it is to happen, so we obsess about things that scare us, even if they are unlikely. We worry about snakes, or getting on airplanes, when the real threats to longevity are cheeseburgers, chocolate shakes and long hours lounging on the couch.

A telling example is how when we think about the future, we want it to be grand. We imagine dramatic positive changes like personal jetpacks and transporter beams, ignoring how every novel and science fiction film of the last 50 years failed to capture the essence of what changes over time and what does not. Simply wanting a cleaner, smarter world for our children doesn't have any impact on how likely it is to happen.

I believe the future, in many ways, will be boring. Much of daily life will be the same as it is now. I don't want this to be the case, but I believe it in spite of my wantings. When I tell people this, they are disappointed. Because I've written books about innovation they expect I'll have great faith in how amazing life will be in the decades to come. This is wrong. I'd love new and better things to happen, but I don't let that influence what I think is likely.

One reason I believe this is the history of ideas. The difference between ideas that change the world, and those that remain on the drawing board, includes large quantities of chance and circumstance. There's no grand reason we have 12 months in a year instead of 15, or 60 seconds in a minute instead of 100. They're just numbers someone made up. Politics, self-interest and conflicting beliefs influence all important decisions made today, just as they did in the past and will in the future. Why the U.S. is one of a handful of countries in the world that doesn't use the metric system has more to do with circumstance than good reason.

Ideas like the golden rule, or pay it forward, may never become popular. Not because people don't want them to be adopted, but because wanting something to be popular can have little bearing on how popular it becomes. And as much as we might want the future to be different in this regard, it's insufficient for believing it will happen.

A kind of wisdom rises when we strip away what we want or don't want from our view of the world. Then we're free to see things more clearly. There are three ways to do this:

- Acknowledge something you hope doesn't happen will happen anyway (death).

- Want something even if it's improbable (developing superpowers as you age).

- Be open to data that disproves the theory you want.

Take a moment to list your beliefs. If you're careful, you'll discover wants lurking inside. It's good to want things and fight for them, but misplaced belief is not the way to wisdom.

HOW TO BE A
FREE THINKER

In the same way a man can be chained to an oak tree, a mind can be chained to an assumption, a religion, or any idea. But the idea, like the tree, should not be blamed. It is inanimate and is good or bad only in how it is used. Instead it's the chain that must be questioned, and the motivations of the people using them. Each mind is unique for its infinite ideas and can be used to think about anything in a thousand ways. Any act that confines a mind to a singular way of thinking cannot be good. And yet all communities, from families, to schools, to gangs, have ideas members are expected to adopt without question. This doesn't make them evil, but it doesn't make them liberators either.

Like the rules to a new board game, we absorb these ideas with our minds at half-power, since our goal is to learn and follow. Traditional education mostly teaches us to copy, to memorize, and apply other people's theories. What does this train us for other than performing these thoughtless behaviors throughout our lives?

And the things that are considered taboo in our societies, acts that violate traditions, are banned without parents, teachers or leaders understanding why. Why is being seen in underwear embarrassing, but in a bathing suit is not? Why are nipples and flesh forbidden to see, when everyone has them? Why are alcohol, nicotine and Prozac legal, but marijuana and Absinthe criminal? It's un-free thinking, this accepting of an idea simply because someone said so. If an idea is good, it will thrive in fair debate and discussion, and if it's weak, it will wither away.

Wisdom demands two questions: Why do we believe what we believe? How do we know what we know? They should be stamped on every schoolbook and posted in every meeting place and home to encourage independent thought. It should be tattooed on the forehead of anyone arrogant enough to dictate orders for others to follow.

When a child asks "why," to every answer, the game often ends with the parent embarrassing the child: "Stop being silly," they say. But they are hiding their own embarrassment. It's harder for them to say "I don't know" despite its truth. Why not be proud of the child's inquisitive mind and hope they ask questions their entire lives? We all know less than we think, and learning it starts by admitting ignorance, and asking more questions, not fewer.

Questions help us discover the ideas that bind us: chains forced upon us as children, before we found the will to refuse and question. Chains we used to bound ourselves, to fit in at school, at work, or with friends. Free thinkers forever seek to acknowledge, understand and disprove their assumptions. They hunger to discover better ideas, wiser opinions, and more worthy faiths. They are willing to abandon ideas they've held dearly, seeking when they learn an important belief has been held for the wrong reasons.

When I first ate Ethiopian food, I asked three times "Are you sure it's ok to eat with my hands?"

It didn't occur to me that a) they're *my* hands, b) it's *my* mouth, and c) I'm paying for the food. Shouldn't I do what I please? For all of America's freedoms, we're still under the tyranny of silverware. When I went to India, I was scolded for eating with my left hand. At a fancy French restaurant, I got dirty looks for eating with the wrong fork. Travel makes clear how arbitrary the rules we defend are. We often have trivial reasons for being offended or judging others.

The first challenge: Be wrong. It's ok.

Brace yourself: you're wrong—much of the time. I'm wrong too and some of this essay will be wrong (except for this sentence). Even if you're brilliant, successful, happy and loved, you're wrong and ignorant more than you realize. It's not your fault. None of our theories are entirely true. This is good. If we had all the answers, progress would be impossible. Look back 100, 50, or even 5 years. Consider the smartest people of those times: weren't they misguided, compared to what we know now? Governments, religions, cultures and traditions all change, despite what they say. Each evolves. Traditions do have value, but ask yourself: who decides what to keep and what to toss? Why did they make these decisions? There are stories of free-thinking and change hiding in every tradition.

What beliefs have you held and discarded? If you have kept the same beliefs and theories your entire life, then you haven't been paying attention. To be wiser, smarter, and more experienced than you were a decade ago means you've changed. It's good to think differently about life than you did before; it's a sign future progress is possible. If you pride yourself on rigid consistency, you bury intelligence under pretense. Only when you're free from allegiance to a specific idea, and put faith in your ability to learn, can progress happen.

The second challenge: other people

Children survive by conformity. By recognizing adult behavior and adjusting to it, they survive. Babies quickly learn that crying bring food and smiles get attention. We're designed for survival not freedom. Consider Buddha's excellent advice:

"Believe nothing, no matter where you read it, or who has said it, even if I have said it, unless it agrees with your reason and your own common sense."

This is the opposite of what adults teach children: teachers test and grade them on their ability to memorize answers. At what point must we teach our children to think for themselves? There are no required college courses called "undoing the damage of the last 18 years of your life" or "how to escape the evil tyranny of your dogmatic education." We're on our own to figure out what freedom means.

Freedom grows best in diversity. Absorb ideas. Compare them. Question them. Challenge them. If you share ideas with only those who agree with your philosophies, you're just sharpening your prejudices. Sharpening prejudices can be fun, but it's not thinking, free or otherwise. Finding safe places to share different ideas is hard to find, so start looking now.

The third challenge: be alone

Many of history's wisest men retreated from their routines for a time. Jesus, Buddha, Moses, and Muhammad all freed themselves from the conventions and commitments of normal life. Only then were they able to discover, to transform, learn and understand themselves in ways that changed the world. They had to break chains and bonds to think freely. Only with new perspective and priorities, did they choose to return. I doubt this choice was popular among those who knew them. Their long absences bothered their children, friends, landlords, and tennis partners.

They say the fish is the last to see the water. But what if the fish could step out of the tank now and then? You're not a fish: you can take that step whenever you like.

When was the last time you were free from others? Can you name the last day you spent alone with your thoughts? Travel, meditation, long baths, a run in the woods—they're all ways to experience the solitude we need to think freely, and to understand ourselves for who we really are. Our heart of hearts, our truest, freest voice, is always talking, but it's timid. We can't hear it over the chatter of everyday life. Make quiet time to learn how to hear it. We're still free to ignore that voice, but only after we have tried to listen. Being free has never been easy, which explains why so few, despite what they say, truly are.

HOW TO DETECT BULLSHIT

Everyone lies: it's just a question of how, when, and why. From the relationship-saving, "you look thin in those pants," to the improbable, "your table will be ready in five minutes," truth manipulation is part of the human condition. Accept it now.

As irrational beings who find it hard to accept tough truths, our deceptions protect us from each other and ourselves. Deceptions help avoid unnecessary conflicts, hiding the confusion of our psychologies from those who don't care. White lies are the spackle of civilization, tucked into the dirty corners our necessary but inflexible idealisms create.

But lies, serious lies, destroy trust, the binding force in all relationships. Bullshit (BS) is a particularly troublesome kind of lie. Bullshit involves unnecessary deceptions, in the gray area between polite white lies and malicious fabrications. The Bullshitters, ignorant of facts, invent a story to protect themselves. They don't mean any harm, although collateral damage often happens. BS can be hard to detect, so this is a crash course in BS detection. But be warned: there are several bits of BS in this essay. You'll have to find them for yourself.

Why people bullshit: a primer

The Western canon's first lie comes from the Old Testament.[1] To recap the book of Genesis, God tells Adam and Eve not to eat fruit from the tree of knowledge, as pretty as it is, or they'll die. God wanders off to do some unexplained godlike things, as gods are prone to do. Meanwhile, the oh-so-tempting tree is out for all to see, without a pack of divine pitbulls or angelic electrified fences to guard it. Satan slinks by and convinces Eve that the fruit of the tree is good: so she and Adam have a snack. God returns instantly and scolds Adam—who blames Eve which results in everyone, snakes, people and all, getting thrown out of Eden forever.

Here, nearly everyone lied. God was deceptively ambiguous, a kind of lie, in the description of the fruit. The fruit wasn't fatal in any sense Adam could understand. If we were Adam, only a few moments old and ignorant of everything, when God mentioned "death" we'd either have no idea what God meant, or would assume the literal kind. Satan misrepresents the fruit's power, and Adam approximates a lie by pointing a wimpy finger at Eve. It's a litany of deception and a cautionary tale: in a book where everyone lies in the first pages, is it a surprise how the rest plays out?

People lie for three reasons. The first is to protect themselves. They wish to protect something they need, such as a concept they cherish, or to prevent something they fear, like confrontation. There is a clear psychological need motivating every lie. A well known fib, "the dog ate my homework," fits this model. Desperate not to be caught, children's imaginations conceive amazing improbabilities: fires, plagues, revolutions, curses and illnesses. They reinvent the laws of physics and

---

[1] One popular interpretation of Genesis 2:17 is that God meant "you will be mortal" when God said "you will surely die," so it's not a lie. My view is how could Adam know what he meant at the time? Even if that's what he meant, I find it hard to believe anyone would interpret it that way.

the space-time continuum on fateful mornings when children find themselves at school, sans-homework. It's an emotional experience, this need to BS: logically speaking, the stress of inventing and maintaining a lie is harder than just telling the truth. Yet we don't.

The second reason people lie? Sometimes it works. It's a gamble, but when we sneak one by, wow. Did you lie to your parents about girls, boys, drugs, grades, or where you were until two a.m.? I sure did and still do. My parents still think I'm a famous painter / doctor in London. (Shhhhh.) My best friend still believes his high school girlfriend and I didn't get it on every time I borrowed his car.[2] Even my ever faithful dog Butch used to lie, in his way. He'd liberate trash from all our garbage cans, then hide in his bed, hoping his distance from the Jackson Pollock esque refuse mess in my kitchen signified innocence.

The third reason we lie? We want others to see us as better than we see ourselves. Sadly, comically, we believe we're alone in this temptation, and the shame it brings. Everyone has weak moments when fear and greed melt our brains tempting us to say the lies we wish were true. The deepest honesty is from those willing to admit to their lies and own the consequences. Not the pretense of the saints, who pretend, incomprehensibly, inhumanly, to never even have those urges at all. But enough philosophy: let's get to detection.

Bullshit detection: how do you know what you know?

The first rule? Expect BS. Fire detectors expect a fire at any moment: they're not optimists. To detect bullshit, you have to question everything you hear. Socrates, the father of Western wisdom, expected ignorance. Like Socrates, assume people,

---

[2] This is, of course, complete bullshit. I have never lied to anyone. Ever.

yourself included, are unaware of their ignorance. You must probe intelligently, and compassionately, to sort out the difference.

When someone force feeds you an idea, an argument or an obscure reference, ask the question: "How do you know what you know?" Challenging claims illuminates ignorance. It instantly diminishes the force of an opinion based in bullshit. Here are some examples:

- "The project will take five weeks." How do you know this? What might go wrong that you haven't accounted for? Would you bet $10,000 on your claim? $100,000?

- "Our design is groundbreaking." Really? Where is that ground? And who, besides the designers/investors, has this opinion?

- "Studies show that liars' pants are flame resistant." What studies? Who ran them and why? Did you actually read the study or a two sentence summary? Are there any studies that make the opposite claim?

Notice your subject often can't answer quickly when you ask: "How do you know what you know?" Even credible thinkers need time to establish their logic and separate assumptions from facts.

Answers such as: "this is purely my opinion" or "it's a guess—we have no data," are fine, but those claims are weak—far weaker than most people make, especially if they're making stuff up. Identifying opinion and speculation counts as progress in the war against deception.

Bullshit detection: what is the counter argument?

A well-considered argument must involve alternate positions, so ask for them. Bullshitters don't do research, they make things up. A counterargument forces them to defend their position or end the discussion to conduct due diligence. Similar questions include: Who else shares this opinion? What are your concerns and how will they be addressed? What would have to happen for you to have a different (opposite) opinion?

Time and pressure

Good thoughts hold together. A solid concept maintains its shape no matter how much you poke, probe, test, and examine it. But bullshit is all surface. Much like a magician's bouquet, it's pretty as it flashes before your eyes, but you know it's fake when it lands in your hands. Bullshitters know this and crave urgency: they resist reviews, breaks, consultations, or sleeping on a decision before it's made.

Use time as an ally. Never make big decisions under duress. Ask to withhold judgment for a day, and watch the response. Invite experts to help make decisions to add intellectual pressure. Hire them if necessary: the $500 lawyer/accountant/consultant fee is bullshit insurance. These habits create inhospitable environments for bullshit.

Confidence in reduction

Jargon and obfuscation hide huge quantities of bullshit. Inflated language intimidates others and is always a tactic to make people feel stupid. If you don't understand something, it's their fault, not yours. Cling to your doubts longer than the bullshitter can maintain their charade.

For example:
"Our dynamic flow capacity matrix has unprecedented downtime resistance protocols."

If you don't understand, err on your own side. Don't assume you're missing something: assume they haven't communicated clearly. They might be hiding something, or maybe they don't know what they're talking about. Wise responses include:

- I refuse to accept this proposal until I, or someone I trust, fully understands it.

- Explain this in simpler terms I can understand (repeat if necessary).

- Break this into pieces you can verify, prove, compare, or demonstrate for me.

Are you trying to say, "our network server has a backup power supply?", If so, can you speak plainly next time?

Assignment of trust

The fourth bullshit-detection tool is to assign trust carefully. Never agree to more than what your trust allows. Who cares how confident they are? The question is: how confident are you? Divide requests, projects or commitments into pieces so people can earn your trust one step at a time. And trust can be delegated. I don't need to trust you if you've earned the trust of people I trust. Nothing defuses BS faster than communities that help each other eliminate BS. Great teams and families help each other find truth, both in others and themselves, as sometimes the real deceptions we need to fear are our own.

SHOULD YOU BE POPULAR OR GOOD?

One of the grand confusions of life is between what is popular and what is good. Often people confuse popularity with goodness, and it's a problem. When we consider the top ten books or movies of the year, we often consider which ones were most popular, but popularity doesn't mean they were necessarily the best. Being popular means appealing to everyone, which demands safe, predictable choices. A good idea scares some people, and makes others uncomfortable, which works against its popularity.

For example, I knew a guy in high school who was very popular, but I don't think anyone would say he was good at anything. He was nice, but bland. I knew another guy in high school who was good at lots of things, but for some reason, he wasn't popular. He spoke his mind and didn't always try to please everyone. I suspect if these two guys ever met, the universe would have exploded. Good thing that didn't happen.

Many creative people are tempted to strive for popularity. They make, do, and say things others like, in the hopes of pleasing them. This motivation is nice. And sometimes the end result is good. But mediocrity is often the result of trying hard to please others. The internal goodness detector of those creative people is disappointed with what they make. Popularity often comes at a price: bland, predictable, and meaningless, instead of interesting, surprising, and meaningful.

And then there are the *artistes*, the people who develop their own sense of what they think is good and insist on striving for it, no matter what anyone says. Provided they don't expect anyone else to care, these people are quite interesting. Although, there is little worse in the world than an artiste who insists on telling you how stupid you are for not seeing their brilliance.

In history, it's interesting how characters like van Gogh, Michelangelo, and Bukowski balanced the popular vs. good challenge. Most famous artists accepted commissions, and in some cases those commissions resulted in their most famous work. For example, da Vinci and Michelangelo had many clients and lived on commission income. If you wonder why much of what you see in museums are portraits of old wealthy people, it's because they're the only ones who could afford to pay for paintings. In other cases, like Bukowski, Henry Miller, and Van Gogh, they rarely compromised, sometimes to their own detriment.

What most creative people want is to be good *and* popular. They want to achieve their own sense of goodness, while at the same time pleasing others.. It's a tightrope. Especially once they've earned some popularity, people tend to want more of the same. And that rarely aligns with a creative person's progressive sense of goodness. So from the creator's standpoint, a few big popular victories early on can put handcuffs on how good they can ever be while still being popular. My first book was on project management, and I suspect for some people, no matter how many books I write on other things, I'll always be the project management guy. And that's ok. It's better than not being popular for anything good at all. I know I want to be popular enough to succeed, but I also expect to fail occasionally if I'm following my own compass for what is good.

How do you balance your sense of good vs. your sense of popular? Do you find clear places where they are in conflict (for example, your client's sense of good vs. your own)? How do you balance this with staying sane? Do you divide your creative energy into "work creative" and "personal creative," giving yourself a safe place to be an artist? Or do you still think popular and good are always the same?

THERE ARE TWO TYPES OF PEOPLE: COMPLEXIFIERS AND SIMPLIFIERS

There are two kinds of people: people that make things complex and people that simplify.

Complexifiers are averse to reduction. Instinctively they turn basic assignments into quagmires, and reject simple ideas until they're buried in layers of abstraction. These people write 25-page specifications when a picture would do and send long e-mails to large mailing lists when one phone call would suffice. When they see x=y, they want to play with it and show their talents, taking pleasure in creating the unnecessary ($23x^*z = 23y^*z$). They take pride in consuming more bandwidth, time, and patience than needed, and they expect rewards for it.

Simplifiers thrive on concision. They look for the 6x=6y in the world, and happily turn it into x=y. They never let their ego get in the way of the short path. When you give them seemingly complicated tasks, they simplify, consolidate, and re-interpret instinctively, naturally seeking the simplest way to achieve what needs to be done. They find ways to communicate complex ideas in simple terms without losing it's essence or power.

I don't know what makes a person fall into either pile, but I know I'd rather spend my time with simplifiers than with complexifiers. Don't you think all the best writers, philosophers, and teachers fit into the simplifier group? I'd write more about this opinion, but then I'd be making things more complex than necessary. And if you have serious complaints about the brevity of this piece, we both know which kind of person you are.

ARE YOU INDIFFERENT?

In high school I had the good fortune of having creative friends. We'd do crazy things like dance in the hallways and make strange movies, thanks to the intellectual indulgences of our teacher, Mr. Reinstein. We'd be loud and silly in busy places where others could see, and there I learned a surprising lesson: when you behave oddly on purpose, others feel more embarrassed than you do. They don't know how to respond, so they leave you alone. As wild and unpopular as we were, we were never picked on or laughed at, because our insanity had liberated us. I learned being bold puts people on their heels.

As an adult I find this distressing. I know, all things being equal, when something interesting is happening people will pretend to be indifferent, even if in their hearts they're interested in what's going on.

Today I was in Pike Place Market, a historic strip of old buildings and shops in Seattle. On the winding stone passageway called Post Alley there were was a series of street musicians. Each had a guitar or banjo and was singing their heart out. Many were good, and I stopped to listen at each one. When I did, pleased with my cheap and unexpected front row seat, I couldn't help but notice all the people walking past who pretended that the musicians and I weren't there.

If some talented person magically appeared in your home or office, and began performing a passionate private concert for you, you'd be moved. It's rare these days to see someone performing a craft live and in person. Yet these musicians performing on the street, putting their full energy out into the world for anyone's pleasure, garnered no reaction. People walked past without a glance, staring at their own shoes, as if they were surrounded by long dead sidewalks.

It's strange how we can spend hours a day behind electric screens of various shapes and sizes, bored by how unreal much of it is, yet walk right past living musicians without a glance. We treat amazing things as if they weren't there.

As I stood listening, I soon felt strange. Why am I the only one here? Even though I knew it was right to stay and listen it felt weird because I was alone. Had there been a crowd around any of the musicians, more people would have stopped to join, simply because they could do it without feeling strange. But standing alone, I felt I was doing something wrong. It's sad, but I'm no longer that crazy kid in high school, running through the hallways. Now I'm more like the others, worried more about standing out than enjoying the world.

I call this the *challenge of indifference*. As we grow up we're taught self-control, how to focus ourselves, and how to tune out things that are "wrong" or "juvenile" or "wastes of time." We become indifferent to the whims of the child mind, trading it in for suits and resumes—the tools of success in the adult world. But success becomes boring. For most knowledge-worker types, life is an abstraction. We move things around we can't hold in our hands, and we get paid for doing dull things for dull people we never meet and never know.

The challenge as an adult, once you've found your way and settled down, is to undo indifference. That's where happiness is: in paying attention in the ways we did when things were new, and we were young enough not to judge. We all have that voice in our heads that whispers, "This is cool" or "This is different" or even "Wait—what is this? Let's see," but it's pounded into submission by the stodgy, stronger, rational adult voice we've used to get the external things we covet so dearly.

I know many people who are fundamentally frustrated with their lives and have been for some time. And they're surprised they feel this way—after all, they're successful at work. They expected that fact to be enough to make them happy forever, as that's the mythical bargain. But we're never told that success often demands indifference to the wonders of the real, or the magic of the ridiculous.

My life was changed by films like *Fight Club* and *American Beauty*, because they show how empty a successful life can be. They expose how we create our own emptiness which can only be filled from the inside out, not with expensive material things. It starts by rediscovering what we overlook, including people living their passions, like street musicians, chefs, or craftsmen, people who are not indifferent. They are fully present, and give us a chance to join them in the moment, but only if we stop to listen.

DOES TRANSPARENCY MATTER?

Whenever people speak of transparency, in governments or corporations, I think of overhead projectors. This dates me significantly, and if you don't know what an overhead projector is, I'll indulge you. Around the dawn of time, professors used to write their lessons on sheets of cellophane called transparencies. They'd put the cellophane on a special box of light, which would be projected onto a screen at the front of the room. This was very clever since the clear sheets projected light around the words and diagrams, making them visible.

Transparency is good for this reason. It lets you see. In many circles today, transparency is a buzzword for goodness. When something is broken, people say "this can be fixed by making it more transparent." For example, in business, if Rupert and Marla can see what the CEO is thinking, or what the actual revenue numbers look like, they'll better understand why they're being asked to do whatever they're doing. And in families, if little Sally and Johnny understand why it's bad for them to consume all their daily calories in the form of Double stuffed Oreos and triple chocolate shakes, they're more likely to honor their parents wishes.

Transparency means clarity. You give access to more information so people can see what is going on and why. The challenge is, the more exposed the inner workings of things are, the more complex they seem. When you look closely at anything for the first time, it's a shock, and most people, most of the time, don't like that experience, despite what they say. When you open something in the name of transparency, it can be disruptive if not done carefully, or if you're dealing with people who can't handle much truth. Ask a physicist what's inside an atom, and very quickly most people realize they'd really rather not know.

Even if plans are well considered and explained, and everyone has the fortitude to accept difficult realities, there is a new problem. What happens if Rupert sees flaws in the CEO's thinking? Or Sally discovers something about nutrition that's new to her parents? Is it acceptable for Rupert to ask questions? Will those in authority accept them respectfully? Will parents incorporate new information that threatens the old?

If not, then the transparency offered is *one way*, which has limited value. For example, if my plan is to do something stupid, say to start a chain of hamster burger franchises, one way transparency with my staff won't improve anything. If the world hates hamster burgers, yet I insist on betting the company on them, the transparency of my plan has little effect on the quality of the business.

The real goal of transparency should be to achieve better thinking. But this doesn't happen because of the transparency itself. Better thinking happens only when leaders listen to feedback, changing their plans to incorporate better ideas.

Those in power have to behave graciously when criticized, and reward people who provide good ideas, not with token praise, but with the only true reward—improving the plan.

When it comes to marketing, transparency is more contrived. Someone selling a product will never say certain things, even if they're true. An advertisement will never claim "This product is not as good as our competitor's", "Our customer service sucks," or "This sounds awesome but no one uses it after it's purchased". Wise consumers know this. We know there are things marketers will never say. And in all communication there are unsaid and fundamental limits to how transparent the message can be.

Media theory often uses the word authenticity, implying some forms of media are more authentic than others. It's the wrong word to use. The web may have humanized sales and marketing, as the personality of people comes through in greater measure. But that's not the same as being authentic. Consider how the words "old fashioned" and "homemade" appear on products made in large, new factories, a practice established by talented marketers. Being authentic requires believing completely in what you say, which is beyond what marketers, public relations and sales professionals do.

Trust is always more important than authenticity and transparency. On the human level, to say "Fred is so transparent" means something negative. We literally mean we see through him to his untrustworthy core. The more I trust you, the less I need to know about the details of your plans or operations. Honesty, diligence, fairness, and clarity are the hallmarks of good relationships of all kinds and lead to the magic of trust. And it's trust that's hardest to earn and easiest to destroy, making it the most precious attribute of all. Becoming more transparent is something you can do by yourself, but trust is something only someone else can give to you. If transparency leads to trust, that's great, but if it doesn't, you have bigger problems to solve.

HOW I FOUND MY PASSION

You can't deliberately find passion. If there is a way, I don't know of it. Throughout the ages the wise have explored this question in a thousand ways, and they've all failed to provide a solution that works for everyone. Most people are passionless about their work, much less their lives, and it makes them unhappy. If there were a simple way to change their lives, they would.

Looking backwards, I see I've tried different things. Over the course of my life I've had opportunities to spend more time doing things I liked to do. The fortunate part is twice I've found ways to make a living doing things I'm passionate about: first with software, now with writing.

But my first love was baseball. It was my father's game and I inherited his joy for the sport's simple pleasures. But by age 10 I discovered basketball, a game of endless movement and changing patterns, and I loved it more. It was the defining passion of my life, something I hoped to do professionally, despite my less than impressive stature. It was here I discovered the value of work. I outworked better athletes and peers with greater physiques. For the first time I saw my training and hard work pay off in results I could not achieve otherwise. When I gave up basketball, I retained an appreciation for effort. I learned I could outwork people who were better than me, provided I converted my passion into work. I'd learn later that all masters in all fields were similarly driven. Call Mozart or Picasso prodigies if you like, but they spent more hours at the piano and the easel than their competitors did.

I started writing junior year of high school. We had a poetry month in English class and I wrote a few poems. To my surprise, I loved it. I can't explain why. The intellectual challenge of putting words in order, and the freedom to take a notion in my mind and manifest it in the world, gave me pleasure. I enjoyed it enough I wrote on my own, and I've continued ever since. During my freshman year of college we had to keep a journal for a philosophy course. Initially I wrote to please the professor, but soon I discovered I enjoyed going back and reading what I had written weeks before. Who was the person who wrote this? And now, in the future, what do I think of what he thought back then? I learned something through this process I couldn't learn any other way, and I've kept it up since.

These three experiences were pivotal in becoming a writer. Had I not learned to see the necessity of work in achievement, and been exposed twice to my own discovery of the pleasure in writing, I would not be writing this now.

I've never believed in the idea of a calling. Most people are good at different things, and can live happy lives in many different ways. If you want to find your passion, put yourself in different situations, with different people, and see how it makes you feel. Pay attention to your own sense of excitement, not others, and write down your responses. Some of what you try will bore you. Some of it you'll hate. You may notice you take pleasure in something, but it's the approval of others that's the source, and not the activity itself. But with each experience you'll have a growing sense of who you are, what you actually care about, and what you're good at doing.

There are four piles of things in the world:

- Things you like/love.

- Things you are good at.

- Things you can be paid to do.

- Things that are important.

But only you can sort out what belongs in each pile, or hopefully, all four piles at the same time.

Growing up, we're fed many stories about what we're supposed to like, or enjoy, or find pleasure in, and only some of that turns out to be true. It's implied you need a great career to be happy, but many people with fancy careers seem miserable. You can't be passionate if you're living your parents' dream and not your own. And to separate the two requires some wandering, some courage, and some time where you know the answer won't come quickly.

My advice is simple: pick something. Do it with all your heart. If you can't keep your heart in it, do something else. Repeat. Your desires will change as you age, and to assume you can do one thing your whole life and be satisfied is foolish. Developing self-knowledge will help you make the next choice, and the next, leading to a passionate life. Few people have the courage to do this, even for a year, much less a lifetime. But my suspicion is, if you ask passionate people how they make choices, this is what you'll hear.

HOW TO BE PASSIONATE

A gentleman named Vijay asked me, after a lecture, how I could have so much energy. He said, "I noticed your energy was explosive and there was no point in the presentation where I detected a lull. I'm interested in learning any secrets in maintaining the focus of not just the audience, but also of yourself."

Explosive energy only makes me think about the short life expectancy of drummers in Spinal Tap. Passion is good, but there's a point where enthusiasm is a distraction. Think of televangelists or telemarketers, they certainly seem passionate, but all it makes you want to do is make them stop. Yet, it's no accident Vijay had that response. It's the response I work hard to generate in people who come to hear me speak.

There are four things that explain what's going on:

1. **My life is at stake.** I have bet I can make a living on my ideas and my ability to express them. I have no guarantees, no salary, and no pension. Every time I write a blog post, publish a book, or give a talk, I'm an entrepreneur. I'm not half invested. This isn't a side

project. THIS IS IT. I need people to buy my books, hire me to speak, and to tell others about me. When you've invested your heart in something, it's much easier to appear passionate about it, because you are.

2. **I believe what I say.** I hate people who water things down, intentionally mislead, or pretend they care about things they don't. How much of what people say at work do they truly believe or care about? I think carefully about what I create, so when the time comes to lecture, my points are things I believe deeply. And I've worked hard to make them clear and concise. I'm not holding back because I know it's easier to get excited about things I believe in, especially if they are crafted down to their essence. However, if you asked me to talk about my favorite tax software, or which 401k forms I liked the most, my passion would be hard to find.

3. **I've extended my range.** If you can only play one note on your guitar, you can't do very much. Musicians, especially singers, practice to extend their range. Most speakers have a narrow range. If you listen carefully to comedians or other great speakers you'll notice how wide their range is. They can whisper (volume level two) or almost holler (volume level eight). They also have a range of natural gestures, postures, and facial expressions. The wider your range, the more tools you have to express passion, humor or anything. You extend your range through practice and coaching. I never want to be too passionate, as it's easy to sound like a preacher on cocaine or a bad infomercial salesman. My ambition is to be a charismatic, but reasonable person, with a high level of genuine enthusiasm.

4. **I honor anyone who listens voluntarily.** Speaking and writing are subjective, and I know reasonable people might not like me, or what I have to say. But the energy

and effort I put in is undeniable. I never want people to dismiss me for not being sincere. They can hate me, prove me wrong, or heckle me, but I don't want anyone leaving the room, or finishing one of my books, feeling like I gave half an effort. Any speaker is burning more calories per second than any listener, but that's often forgotten by those judging from the back row, where it's safe to believe they could easily do better.

PART TWO
SPARKS

ON GOD
AND INTEGRITY

In 1991 I watched my team, the New York Giants, hold on to a small lead in the closing minutes of Super Bowl XXV. They were up by one point, and with eight seconds left the Bills had a chance to win the game by kicking a field goal. It's a horrible feeling to have your fate entirely in the hands of your competitor. And I hated that long pause, the announcers rambling on, while waiting for the kick. But something happened in those moments that made it much worse.

Before the Bills kicked the ball, the TV showed the Giants' sideline. A circle of players were huddled together in prayer. Praying for what, I wondered. For the kicker to miss? Yes, indeed. At the time, despite my ignorance of theology, I found this troubling. What kind of god would honor a prayer not only as selfish as this one, but at the expense of someone else? If the kicker missed he'd be hated forever for losing the Super Bowl, a worse fate than anything the Giants players would feel, watching the kicker work from the sidelines.

I wondered what would happen if an equal number of equally faithful Bills players prayed just as piously on the other side of the field. Can you out pray someone? Is that how prayer works? I wondered how an intelligent, attentive, loving god could make decisions such as this. By counting prayers? And wouldn't you have to consider, if this is prayer warfare, what the other team's prayer strategy was before kneeling down to pray for your own team? A drop of logic makes all this fade into foolishness, as the machinery by which these acts affect life defies any reasonable person's imagination.

As it turned out, Scott Norwood, the Bills kicker, missed the kick. And as predicted, despite a great career he is best known for one kick he missed. My Giants won the Super Bowl and I was happy. But as much as I'd wanted this outcome all season, there was something wrong. A win is not the same as the other team losing by making a mistake, or missing an easy shot. The last seconds of this game often makes the list of greatest Super Bowl moments in history, but it's not for me. I put myself in the kicker's shoes every time.

I don't have problems with the idea of God, or faith in God. I have an open mind and am open to many kinds of ideas. But I do have a problem when the name of God is used to justify behavior that runs against human integrity. Take, for instance, the Golden Rule. I like the Golden Rule. It's a core idea in nearly every religion, nation, culture, or tribe, and I see it as a kind of integrity and basic ethic. I will treat others in the same way I wish to be treated (or as I understand they want to be treated).

Many of the Ten Commandments and similar moral codes in other cultures are implementations of the Golden Rule's core theme. But to pray for victory, without considering that the people on the other side might also be fans of your flavor of god, or even if not fans of your flavor they are still people worthy of your respect, cannot be an act of integrity. No one would want a competitor with God's ear to ask for their failure. The whole idea makes God a possession – MY GOD. A god who is here to help me and my needs. Rather than, OUR GOD. A god that has the collective interest of all life, or human life, in mind. When anyone claims sole dominion over spiritual territory for their personal gain, claiming VIP access to the deities, it's sure to send everyone involved straight to hell (metaphoric or literal depending on your beliefs).

The only high integrity prayer, or act, is to hope that the team that plays best, wins. Or to wish that everyone plays well, and that no one gets hurt. And like the Klingons and their wish for a noble death (they don't mind losing their lives provided it happens in the right way), that in the end everyone can walk off the field feeling proud because they played well and hard, and gave it their best. That even if they lost, they feel there's nothing else they could have done. As a competitor that is the most noble outcome of all: everyone played well and was at their best.

I have similar questions when I see a star athlete point to the sky when they win. What exactly is this intended to mean? I'm a fan of humility, and giving thanks to people, life, the universe at large, or anything really, but it's not clear this is what's happening. Would they point to the sky if they lost? Isn't God, or whatever they're pointing to, up above in all cases, regardless of the outcome? If they catch a winning touchdown pass, shouldn't they point at least a little bit to the guy who threw the ball? Or the coach who put them on the field?

A better demonstration of devotion, faith, or humility, is what you do when there is no spotlight on you. Or, as often happens in life, you are not the center of attention for a big reward, and instead are in the crowds with the rest of us, with plenty of disappointment around you. What do you do then? Who do you point to and what does it mean? Or more precisely, how generous and humble are you in your treatment of others in and below your station then? The essence of people, whether you call it spirit, soul or integrity, is found out of the spotlight and the glory. When I'm able to remember this I find heroes and saints worthy of emulation without needing someone else to point them out for me, or draw attention to themselves by pointing up to the heavens.

HATING VS LOVING

A book that changed my life was *Living, Loving and Learning*, by Leo F. Buscaglia. It taught me I was doing things that made me, and those around me, unhappy. One of my big crimes was feeling more comfortable hating than loving.

Any time you hate something there is a choice. You can focus on the hate, outrage, and self-righteousness, or you can find the opposite of the thing you hate, and focus on loving that more.

If you betray me as a friend, I could fixate on how much I hate you, or I can think about my friends who have never betrayed me, and go thank and honor them. Why focus on how much you hate a book, when you can easily remember and share other books you love? If that friend or book disappointed you so much, why not use that energy to appreciate the good you now realize you're lucky to have?

Hate is easy. Destroying things takes much less effort than making them—always has and always will. Hate is also less fulfilling and more isolating than love, since it says what something is not, instead of what it is or could be. Boycotting and banning are attempts to stop something, and stopping bad things is good – but these activities always make me think: why not use that energy to go support something good that deserve move love?

In many cultures, hate, and angry criticism, is safer to express than love (e.g., American men prove they're close friends by finding funny insults for each other, rather than ever saying how much they care for each other). It's common in repressed, dysfunctional groups to confuse hate and criticism with love when that is the primary emotion parents or leaders provide – after all, hating is still a kind of attention. Kids are genetically programmed to believe their parents love them, so if all they get is hate when they're young, they equate hate with what should have been love, and often wander through life confused about what a healthy relationship feels like. In some workplaces the dynamics are similar. If all you know is judgment, that's all you'll express even when you're trying to love, and on it goes.

I learned something important from Buscaglia's book, which I'd never believed before. People who love openly, especially in the face of those quick with anger and snarky sarcasm, are the bravest and most positive forces our species has. You'll always find many people happy to hate in the open, but you can't negate hate with hate. What you can do is turn it around, or slow hate down, with the genuine expression of positive love. Only when hate is out of the way can progress start to happen.

I'm not saying suppress hate. I'm still a hateful bastard now and then. It's therapeutic, it's fun and can be a way to bond with someone for the first time – but I've become careful not to let hate define my character. If I hate something, once I'm done tearing it to shreds, I force myself to look for something with the opposite traits of that thing I hate and show it some love. I can't express how profoundly this has changed my life for the better.

MY SURPRISE INSPIRATION: DEATH

I know this sounds morbidly strange, but when I'm bored or frustrated or out of sorts, thinking about dying inspires me. When I realize I will die and imagine the sensation of everything I feel, think and know of myself to be gone, my senses vibrate in a way I can't explain. It's a long shot to be alive at all, and here I am, born at a time and place where I have millions of choices. I can read any book, see any movie, visit any art, make, do, and feel more things than 99% of all humans who have ever lived. It's all waiting for me, right NOW. Confronting the notion of the end of my own life—as far away as I'd like that to be—is the most reliable way to get inspired. By comparison, to sit and watch TV or wallow in my own hubristic complaints seems unbelievably dumb. And I don't like to feel dumb.

Kafka wrote "The meaning of life is that it ends." Every one of my choices matters because I won't have them forever. Jim

Morrision said "I want to get my kicks in before the whole shithouse goes up in flames." Horace wrote "Carpe Diem!" If I'm not getting what I want out of my life while I'm alive, or giving to those in need, or who I care about before I kick the bucket, when do I expect to do it?

So there it is. I confess, I'm moved by the idea of my own death and I think about it often. I want to die regret-free and the thought of confronting my last moments having to justify being bored with my own memory of my own life compels me to passionately appreciate the choices I make today.

BONUS: YOUR QUOTA OF WORRY AND HOW TO SHRINK IT

We all have a worrying quota: an amount of worry we are compelled to apply to the world. If our lives get safe, and there isn't much worth worrying about, we fill up our quota by worrying about things that don't really matter much at all. Case in point: I once had an extended conversation with my brother about the criteria for accepting Facebook friend requests from people who were jerks in grade school 25 years ago. Boy – do we need other things to fill our worry quota.

I catch myself worrying about ridiculous, trival things now and then, and the trick that helps, that shrinks my worrying quota is Maslow's hierarchy of needs. Food, water, shelter and warmth are worth worrying about. Not much else. Family and close friends are important and worthy of concern, but the majority of details that constitute our daily worry are unworthy.

Sometimes decisions are so insignificant that simply flipping a coin to decide and get the decision out of the way is the best and healthiest thing all around. Neither end of the decision matters provided a decision is made. The only bad choice is taking too much time to make one. I shrink my worry quota by a) realizing some decisions matter less than I think, b) reminding myself worrying rarely helps me make better decisions c) getting someone else to confirm I'm worrying too much about something and need to move on.

There are many things in life that generate fear, but how many of them, after the thing we feared has passed, were worthy of that fear?

HOW TO MAKE A DIFFERENCE

I know you care about something: whether it's a person, a place or an idea. I also know whatever it is you care about is something you want to help. You prefer to be useful and to act in service of that friend or concept, rather than against it. These two points mean some actions serve you more than others: the more aligned your cares and actions are, the bigger the difference you make. You don't need to candystripe a cancer ward or be nice to your strange uncle, or his weird kids. To make a difference you simply need to question the value of what you're doing and do something about your answers.

The ego vs. things that matter

When someone starts talking about changing the world or radically reinventing something, odds are good he's talking from his ego, not his heart. Unless he's working on bringing safety to the scared, health to the sick, or opportunity to the poor, the reinvention serves a want (or an ego), not a need. Technology has diminishing returns when it comes to making a difference. Look back at the thing you care about: your friend, your family, your favorite pair of underwear, the idea of free thought—whatever it is. Now think of yesterday and the last few days before that. Did you spend those hours with the things you hold most high? Was the reason you did, or did not, dependent on a technology? I doubt it.

Progress isn't as dependent on technology as it used to be: now it's the use of technology that matters more than technology itself. Since the telegraph we've been sending bits of data to far away places, and we've gotten better at that every year since. But where we're behind is in the quality of what we send each other and how little difference it makes.

For example, here are some problems whose solutions are independent of recent technological advances:

1. You don't know your neighbors.

2. Its been ages since you helped someone just because they needed it.

3. Your spouse thinks you smell funny.

4. You haven't spoken to good friends in months.

5. You're unhappy, burned out, or bored with your life.

6. You've fallen and can't get up.

Everyone I know who designed something that millions of people use, a website or TV show, has trouble connecting that accomplishment with difference making. It's often their first answer, but one they quickly abandon when you ask them about what is most important in their life, or best for the world. Most people talk of similar things: helping family, standing up for something they believe in, sharing an unspoken truth they know others would benefit to hear. These are old and universal themes, things we've wanted to achieve for centuries, and will still want to achieve in the centuries to come.

Forgotten things

On my last day at Microsoft I was invited (thanks to Surya Vanka) to do a final lecture. It was a wonderful event and I talked about important things to a friendly crowd. Afterwards, a peer I respected but didn't know walked my way. He thanked me for the work I'd done. I asked why he'd never said anything before. He told me (get this) that he thought I already knew. He figured I probably heard that all the time. In essence, he didn't want to annoy me with praise. Annoy me with praise! It made me think about how many times I'd seen or read things that mattered to me, yet how rarely I'd offered any praise in return. How infrequently I'd written a review on amazon.com, or left a comment on a blog. I'd done the same thing to many others that this fellow had done to me.

I thought of books I loved, lectures I enjoyed, and good advice I've received, that I never acknowledged to the person responsible. I thought of dozens of people who said honest things that changed me for the better, or who stuck up for me when others didn't, who never knew the impact of their words. I was less than the man who thanked me at my own lecture. He did something about what mattered to him. He walked straight up, looked me in the eye, and offered his thanks, which was something, I realized, I didn't know how to do.

These little forgotten things, an e-mail, a comment, a handshake and a thank you, were not things I'd ever learned. And I realized, I'd inherently believed offering praise in those contexts lessened me. That to compliment was to admit a kind of failure in myself. What a fool I've been, for it takes a better man to acknowledge goodness in others than it does to merely be good. Anyone can criticize or accept praise, but initiating a positive exchange is a hallmark of a difference maker. We assume others make these gestures so we don't have to, but often we're wrong.

The gift of time

I buy more things than I make. I used to think this was a sign of progress, but today I'm doubtful. When it comes to difference making, there's another criterion. Money can come and go, but my time on this planet is finite. How I spend my time, or who I spend it with means more than anything else in my universe. From at least the selfish view, giving my time is the most valuable gift I can give. A $50 gift certificate is worth 60 seconds of my time. But a thoughtful personal letter, that costs $2 in goods, will take an hour to write. Which is the more potent gift?

When it comes to what I care about, I have to ask how much of my time, the ultimate commodity, I give. An hour a day? A day a week? A week a year? How many of my remaining minutes on this curious little planet will I invest in what matters most? How many things do I claim to care about, but haven't spent time on in years? Decades? Ever?

Maybe instead of buying things as gifts for people, a financial transaction rather than temporal, I can make them dinner at my home—give them the gift of shared time. Or a night at the theater while babysitting their kids. How about being a babysitter for a day, or a gift certificate for an hour of my time to do whatever they ask me to do. Money and things sure are nice but the more personal choices make the largest possible difference.

Nothing is small

We all have limits. We can't change things as much as we'd like. But we can all do small things that make more of a difference than we realize. If I get good service at a bar, I can write a sweet note on the check about how great the service was. If I can't spare the cash for a big tip, I still spare 15 seconds for thoughtful words written in ink. Or I can look the bartender in the eye and thank her for giving me the best service I'd had all day (an award we can all give daily). A small act of acknowledgment might be the nicest experience they have all week.

I'm the only one who can reinforce what matters to me in the universe. And if my praise and rewards aren't accepted, or if it means less to others than to me, that's fine. It still keeps my cares and behaviors consistent. I can look anyone in the eye and say I am who I think I am. But the odds are good small acts are significant to others. If a musician makes a song heard by 5,000 people, maybe 2,500 will listen and remember. Perhaps 10% will bother to tell anyone else. And of those few how many will actually give it a try, and of those, how many will tell the musician they enjoyed what he made? Of 5,000 people who heard the song, perhaps 10 will return something of thanks to the maker. That's less than 1%. And that's for someone successful enough to sell thousands of what they made.

I'm pledging here to thank people who do things I value. For starters, thanks for reading. If you've bought my books, thanks for buying. From now on I'll leave funny thank you notes, buy anonymous flowers, shake hands, and be a difference maker in the small world that is my own mind. None of what I've written may matter to you, but I hope you'll consider what does and do something about it.

WHY YOU MUST LEAD OR FOLLOW

It's curious what happens when we confront things we dislike. Instead of useful choices, such as taking action or accepting things as they are, we often sit on our asses, point fingers and complain. We're frequently passive, going through life as spectators, rather than creators or supporters. We all have a daily ratio of participating to spectating, and it's higher than we like to admit.

And when it comes to making things with other people, active roles define the difference between making things we're proud of and things we're not. The dictum "lead or follow" means you have to decide for yourself where you stand. If you are committed to something, you need to focus either on leading others, or supporting someone who is.

Leaders vs. followers

Binary logic is popular. We love to divide the world into various kinds of two order piles: good and evil, happy and sad, flowers and weeds, us and them. I'm frustrated by false dichotomies, because I've noticed the universe, when you go outside and have a look around, isn't organized into two piles for anything. The universe is multifaceted and defies dichotomy. Yet dividing things into two piles (as I'm doing in this essay) helps us feel confident in our actions. Provided we choose division for the right reasons and at the right times, it's useful. We just can't forget that the world itself isn't divided, only our view of the world is.

Any time, in any task, we are either leading or following. As a rule of thumb, if you're not sure what you're doing, you're following. Given this division in most work a small number of people are leaders, and a larger number are followers. This can be strictly hierarchical (e.g. Napoleon's army) with fixed roles, or organic, as say in a friend's garage band, where on any given day a different person might lead.

When someone is leading, and doing it well, the most valuable thing for others to do is to get behind their effort. A smart capable leader can only be effective if there are other capable people that choose to put their energy behind the leader's decisions. Every Captain Kirk needs a Mr. Spock and a Dr. McCoy. And it follows that when you're surrounded by people who only seem capable of following, the best action to take, if your goal is progress, is to behave like a leader, giving them someone to put their energy behind.

How to lead

People fear leadership roles because they require visibility and vulnerability. It's impossible to lead without putting yourself, and your point of view, out for everyone else to see. This is why many people don't want to be leaders, despite how easily they criticize whoever is in charge. Even people who have jobs that require leadership—executives, managers, senators — often hate the parts of the job that involve real leadership action. They're afraid of revealing themselves to others and are uncomfortable with being accountable for decisions that effect other people.

Good leaders are rare. Most people in jobs requiring leadership fail to provide it. Leading means that you shape your opinions and decisions around the greater good of the project you are responsible for. This requires sacrificing your own interests and wants in favor of the project's needs, and the people who work on it. Of course it's possible to find ways to match your interests with the needs of the project, but it's the project, and the people on it, that comes first.

Good leaders cultivate positive power from others. They use persuasion, intellect, magic spells, free cookies, humor, political acumen, and surprising forms of generosity. Regardless of how, leaders get people to contribute their own energy. It's rarely forced or authority driven. They figure out how to help people cultivate their own internal motivation for what is a good use of their time. And this isn't done through big speeches and morale events: it's a belief built slowly, over time, through each conversation the leader participates in.

Leadership rarely means forcing control over decisions. The value of a leader is their positive effect on a team, not the force and power they have at their disposal. Focusing on the former makes good things happen, but focusing on the latter (force and power) suggests empire building. Some in leadership roles act primarily as though they are in an arms race with everyone else, with little sense of what to use that power for should they ever win their political wars.

How to follow a good leader

If you choose not to lead, or are in a situation where there is another person leading, you are a follower. This doesn't make you a lemming, nor does it require brainwashing, lobotomies, or heavy doses of livestock sedatives. It means your role is to contribute in response to the actions of the leader. Offering your own recommendations, advice, suggestions, and plans might be a large part of your role, provided it's something that both you and the person in the leadership role are comfortable with.

If you are respected by your peers, your supportive acts for a leader can change the balance, transforming a failure into a success. If a leader is doing a good job, the thing the organization needs most from you is to execute and deliver— even if you happen to possess good leadership skills, possibly better than the current leader. If that's not the role you're playing, trying to exercise them anyway can be destructive. You may be trying to prove something to yourself, but in doing so, you can disrupt the flow of decision making, and slow progress.

If you find yourself frustrated by the limits of your role, don't take the passive-aggressive route (e.g., turning meetings into battlefields). Instead, be a leader and find a mature way to handle the situation. If the leader is smart they'll consider making adjustments to give you more responsibility, and plan future changes (or checkpoints to discuss the issue) over the upcoming weeks. If you don't feel they're interested in getting more value from you, you know where you stand. You can choose to stay in the role you have, or move on. But everyone is best served by you choosing to lead or follow. If you choose to lead, and can't lead where you are, go somewhere else.

If you choose to follow, and come across conflicts in carrying out work, or you find problems that the leader didn't account for, it's of course your responsibility to resolve them. Good leaders realize there are things they won't like to hear that they need to hear, and that they need people like you to tell them. They should make it comfortable for you to report bad news, or privately criticize how things are going. Good leaders involve everyone in leadership, and the more leadership skills you have, the more opportunities a smart leader will provide you with for sharing it with the team.

WHY THE WORLD IS A MESS: A THEORY

I have two observations that explain why the world is not going well. These observations apply to families, groups, companies, countries and cultures.

1. **People don't listen.** It's rare for people to genuinely try to understand what others are trying to say. Instead they're waiting for their own chance to speak. And the fact that people aren't listening makes the person speaking feel like they're not being heard, compelling them to talk louder. But talking louder mostly makes people want to listen less, so the negative feedback loop ensues, leading to anger, rage, and rash acts, all motivated by the absence of acknowledgment, not the facts being argued. When you meet an angry person, odds are good they're seeking to be heard, to be acknowledged in some simple way. They don't know how to get it so they act out. It's amazing how people's behavior changes when they feel someone is truly listening.

2. **People don't read.** Coming in at number six in the Ten Commandments, is "Thou shalt not kill". Since it's just past the halfway mark on the list, we can assume most people on planet Earth who are Jewish, Christian or Islamic, know of it. This hasn't had much effect on reducing killing, as plenty of bloodshed has happened by people claiming to upholding their sacred texts, while killing other people who mostly uphold similar sacred texts (all three religions share some theology). Either we don't read the things we claim we do, or we read them with incompetence, preventing ideas in the book from changing our behavior.

This leads to the following conclusions:

1. **If people read more carefully they'd get more of what they want**, as there's a chance they'll recognize that they're looking for the wrong thing. As a writer, my job is to write clearly, but there's only so much a writer can do.

2. **We assume we're listening and reading more**, what with TV, books, and the web, but it's an illusion. It's more acceptable than ever not to listen, as we stare into our phones during meetings and lunches, and merely skim emails and blogs. Within any culture, team, family, or country, where you find more authentic listening and reading, people will be happier, more connected and more successful at achieving things that matter.

When you see people in trouble ask two questions. Who isn't listening? And who isn't reading?

THE SIZE OF IDEAS

We are preoccupied by the size of things: big cars, big sandwiches, and big salaries. In dreams, and in the bestselling books we buy, we seek grand thoughts. The logic we use is the bigger the idea, the bigger the value, but often that's not true. There's a myth at work here, an assumption that big results only come from radical changes. However, there's good evidence for a counter-argument. The problems that hold people back from greatness are often small things, consistently overlooked. The problem is a simple idea that's is rejected by ignorance, lack of discipline or ordinary incompetence. If those simpler, smaller, ideas were set free, the effect would be as potent as any grand theory. Yet somehow we discount simple ideas for being playthings, for being too small to be worthy, dismissing the surprising power hidden in our smallest decisions.

Unlike today's version, the original McDonald's hamburger from 1940 was simple to make. The McDonalds brothers started with a simple idea as owners of several ordinary hamburger stands in San Bernardino, California. As any reasonable owners would do, they explored ways to run those stands efficiently. They tried to make the process for making food repeatable, an assembly line for food construction. Any homemaker or line cook of the 1950s made the same discovery, as making school lunches, or eggs over easy, again and again motivates this kind of thinking. Had you shown the McDonalds' business plan to any of the great business minds of the day, they'd have thought you were insane: they'd have said the idea wasn't big enough to warrant interest of any kind. Fifty years later, McDonalds has 30,000 locations and $22 billion annually in revenue. Certainly not all of that value can be attributed to the simple notion of creative efficiency, but dedication to the notion did enable their early domination of competitors. The point is simple: a small idea, applied consistently, can have disproportionately large effects. Ray Kroc's insight was not finding a big idea, but in seeing how a little idea, done right, could become big.

Put another way, what I'm describing is leverage. Rather than worrying about the size of an idea, which most people do, it's more productive to think about the possible leverage an idea has. Doing this requires thinking not only about the idea itself, but how it will be used. An idea can have a different amount of leverage depending on where, when and how carefully it is applied. One old idea from someone you know, reused in the right way in a different situation, might just have transformative effects. In Atul Gawande's book *The Checklist Manifesto*, he explains how the simple idea of a task list, something used by aircraft pilots for decades, has improved patient safety in surgery by 30% or more. Hospitals didn't need a breakthrough technology. There wasn't a new theory or grand vision. A simple act, with a simple, old tool, had incredible, and surprising, leverage.

There are many dubious stories in the history of ideas, and some, despite their improbability, make valid points. One such story is about Charles Steinmetz (or Edison, or Tesla, depending on the version you hear), holder of more than 200 patents, who retired from General Electric. A complex system had broken, and no one could fix it so they hired him back to consult. Steinmetz found the malfunctioning part and marked it with a piece of chalk. He submitted a bill for $10,000. The GE managers were stunned and asked for an itemized invoice. He sent back the following: *Making the chalk mark $1, Knowing where to place the chalk mark $9,999.* Ideas are like chalk marks: as simple as they seem, knowing where, when, and why to use even the smallest ones can make all the difference in the world.

BOOK SMARTS VS STREET SMARTS

There is no doubt in my mind that street smarts kick book smarts' ass. To be street smart means you have situational awareness. You can assess the environment you're in, who's in it, and the available angles. Being on the street, or in the trenches, or whichever low-to-the-ground metaphor you prefer, requires you learn to trust your own judgment about people and what matters. This skill is of great value everywhere in life regardless of how far from the streets you are.

Most importantly, street smarts come from experience. It means you've learned how to take what's happened to you, good or bad, consider it, and improve. The prime distinction between street smarts and book smarts is who is at the center of the knowledge. On the street, it's you. In a book, you're absorbing someone else's take on the world. However amazing the writer is, you are at best one degree removed from the actual experience. Street smarts means you put yourself at risk and survived. Or thrived. Or have scars. You've been tested and have a bank of courage to depend on when you are tested again. Being street smart can lead to book smarts, as street smart people sense what works and what doesn't, and adapt accordingly.

Book smarts, as I've framed it, means someone who is good at following the rules. There are people who get straight As, sit in the front, and perhaps enjoy crossword puzzles. They like things that have singular right answers. They like to believe the volume, and precision of their knowledge can somehow compensate for their lack of experience applying it in the real world. Thinking about things has value, but imagining how you will handle a tough situation is a world away from actually being in one. (As Tyler Durden says in *Fight Club* – "How much can you know about yourself if you've never been in a fight?")

Like the stereotypical ROTC idiot in war movies (e.g., *The Thin Red Line, Aliens*) who outranks the much more competent and experienced, but less pedigreed sergeant, the book smart confuse pretense with reality, and only learn of the difference after it is too late. Or worse, even after the fact, they insist on seeking out more books and degrees rather than recognizing they are trying to improve the wrong skills: they are half blind by their own choice since they insist on looking at the world with only one eye.

WHY DOES FAITH MATTER?

Why do people think it is important whether or not you believe in God? For a private belief, it has very public consequences in most cultures. There are many reasons faith matters and I have faith my thoughts on them will get me in trouble.

Faith is not a choice for many. Most people mostly believe what their parents believed. Often this is fine, but for some it's a problem, especially if you're the kind of person who realizes if everyone in history believed only what their parents did, we'd still be living in the dark ages, or stuck in the trees in Africa, dreaming of fire. Religious faith matters for many reasons, but one is tradition. We are social creatures and use traditions of many kinds to form families, tribes, cultures and nations. Historically there was little separation between religion and culture, meaning most traditions, and cultural binding forces, were religious. We do things our parents did, from celebrating holidays, to rooting for the same sports teams (a quasi-religion), for the simple reason it's a way for us to connect. Unless there is separation between culture and religion, people will be encouraged to share their parents' beliefs – never exploring their own.

Faith, or even the pretense of faith found in empty religious practice ("I'm an angel on Sunday, and a devil in-between,"), can serve tradition. Saying "I believe in X ," or asking "Why do I believe in X but not Y" when your entire family, or town, believes in Z, requires courage and self-knowledge, which few have. You'd have to risk all you care about to explore a new belief, which is scary. It's safer to avoid questions, or to pretend and keep your beliefs to yourself.

Faith can be useful. My grandmother used to say, when she did something clumsy, "the devil made me do it." Now that's not faith, nor was it an apology. Hell, she didn't even believe in the devil (and probably not in God either), so why say something like this? Believing in something larger than yourself, whether it's a person, a team, a nation, or a god, is empowering. It makes you feel part of something and that you're not alone. As in my grandmother's case, it can also give you someone to blame. Saying "God has a plan" when you know for sure you don't have one, gives relief. And relief can be useful. Feeling connected and empowered can be useful too. But the fact that faith is useful doesn't, on its own, mean the thing you have faith in is real.

There's a saying, "there are no atheists in foxholes" – but that's an awful argument for faith. A person in a crisis is capable of many behaviors, including some bad, self-serving or even self-destructive things. I'm sure there are few pacifists, heroes and lovers, in foxholes too. A better question might be who created the need for the foxholes, and what they claimed to believe.

We are creatures of belief. We are good at believing things. We think in terms of stories and we will invent stories to satisfy our minds, even if those stories are sketchy. The history of progress is us telling increasingly better stories about how things in the world work. We will never get it completely right, and we'll have to admit the stories we believe in now (including those about science) have flaws if we believe in the idea of progress. Either way, we believe. It's what we do. People make fun of the main character in the movie *Memento*, as if, ha ha, we're so much smarter than he is, but we're not. We know, from optical illusions, to Cognitive Bias, that our minds don't work nearly as well as we think they do. Memories are fragile and unstable, despite our intense sense of their permanence. We are masters at coming up with stories to cover up the gaps, and for inventing reasons that conveniently explain, in positive terms, why things happen the way they do. We even manipulate what we remember. We forget that we do it (as it doesn't fit our story of ourselves), but we do.

I believe in many things, because I'm human and I'm alive. It's an evolutionary advantage to be good at believing things. Sometimes I think I'm more successful, or happier, than some other people primarily because I'm better at believing in certain things than they are (it's hard to prove this, but I believe it anyway). But since faith is a specific kind of belief, we are entirely capable of believing faith is good for us, regardless of whether it is or it isn't. If that's a belief you like, you'll find ways to tell yourself stories that reinforce your own emphasis on faith. Since faith is dominant in the history of civilization, it's the default answer. People who choose other beliefs are the minority and therefore have to spend more time justifying their beliefs.

Discussing deism improves discussions of faith. Deism is the idea there is an omnipotent god-like thing, but it doesn't mess with us, and doesn't ascribe to any particular religion (as some flavors of deism go, religions, and their miracles, are inventions). Some of the U.S. founding fathers were likely deists, or had deists notions at one time – possibly Jefferson, Washington, Paine – as it was a popular belief among intellectuals. Deism suggests you can have faith god exists, without the specific beliefs religions tend to assign to that faith. This is powerful, because it separates the existence of God from the ideas of any singular religion.

Even if you think deism is silly, or offensive, follow the exercise – if deists are right, the origins of any religion, and religious scripture, are worthy of investigation. And investigations should be done by sources other than leaders in the religions themselves (who have the most to protect). Perhaps a council of religious inquiry, led by leaders in every major belief who wish to contribute. Or academics and professors of religious history. Suddenly there are explorations that don't discount faith as a concept, but instead examine the pieces with a clear eye. The notion of deism led me to study the history of many religions, which transformed me. There is so much shared between religions, but this rarely fits the dogmatic story you hear from within any particular religion.

There are non-religious kinds of faith. We have faith in gravity, faith in our neighbor, faith that our hearts will keep beating, faith our dog won't raid the kitchen pantry when we go to work. These kinds of faith might have more evidence to back them up in daily life than religious faith, but anyone with complete certainty about anything hasn't been paying attention. I think most people's reasons for believing in most things are dubious. I know plenty of atheists who are just as dogmatic in their atheism as the born-again Christians they criticize.

People who are good to one another and good to themselves are very hard to find, regardless of what scripture they recite or the symbol that hangs from their neck. Above all, I have faith in judging people by their behavior, rather than what they claim to believe, as it's surprising how far apart they often are.

CAN YOU BE GREAT, WITH GRACE?

I've thought about greatness many times, but I can't recall the last time I've seen a magazine or TV show explore the idea. In talking this over with friends, the first question to arise was how to be great, without being unbearable. Many of the names of great people in history have stories loaded with strife, discord, arrogance and ego.

The easy definitions of greatness focus on external achievement. These are people who cure diseases, lead nations, pioneer progress, earn great wealth, or inspire others. I've read many biographies about people who qualify, and it turns out being driven often makes people hard to like. Some were estranged from their families (Woody Guthrie), had difficult marriages (too many to count), behaved unethically (any robber barons of the 19th, 20th or 21st centuries) and treated co-workers, partners or subordinates poorly. Edison ignored his kids. Steve Jobs and Bill Gates were notorious for yelling at coworkers. Examine any list of greats and you'll find many were mean, immature or depressive, despite their legendary success.

It's surprisingly hard to find people who:

1. Achieved great things for the world

2. Were happy

3. Treated people closest to them well

Can you think of people who meet these criteria? And not based entirely on the movie version of their lives?

This raises a bigger question: are the truly great people the ones whose names we'll never know?

For someone to be a household name during their lifetime, they're likely fame seekers. Prolonged fame is unlikely to be accidental, as wealth makes it easy to hide from cameras. This means the names of great people we know are the ones who chose to put continual energy into being perceived as great, and the books and movies we know are likely about people egotistical enough to try to be seen as great. These are people who obsessed about how the world saw them, perhaps at the expense of how their children, their partners, and their community did.

Perhaps true greatness, or a truly great person, is someone who does the right things for the right reasons without expecting grand rewards. They don't do things "to be the best" or "to be famous" or "to be a legend." Instead they sacrifice those ambitions in favor of simply doing what people around them need. They want to be great only through being useful to those they care about most, regardless of how little acclaim they get from the whole wide world for it.

It might be that the dedicated policeman, the passionate history teacher, the devoted great mom/dad, the wonderful uncle, are the people who are truly great, because they add value to the world for its own reason. While anyone can make a billion dollars, they know only they can raise this child, teach that student, support this community, or help that friend in times of need. And unlike the worldly kind of greatness, spread wide and thin across thousands of people, it might only be humble greatness that runs deep enough into people's hearts and memories, to inspire them for the better, forever.

PART THREE
FIRE

HOW TO GIVE AND RECEIVE CRITICISM

Good feedback is rare. It can take a long time to find people who know how to provide useful criticism, instead of simply telling you about all the things they think are "wrong" with you or whatever you've made. A good critic spends as much energy describing what something is, as well as what it isn't. Good criticism serves one purpose: to give the creator of the work more perspective to help them make their next set of choices. Bad criticism uses someone else's work to make the critic feel smart, superior or better about themselves: things that do nothing to help the recipient of the critique (or in the case of movie reviews, the reader of the critique). Given the difficultly of creative work, it would seem that giving and receiving useful feedback should be an important part of what designers, writers, programmers, and others are taught to do.

Assumptions bad critics make

There are four fundamental assumptions bad critics make:

1. There is one universal and objective measure of how

good or bad something is.

2. That the critic is in sole possession of this measurement skill.

3. Anyone that doesn't possess this skill (including the creator of the work) is an idiot and should be ridiculed.

4. Valid criticisms can and should always be resolved.

Let's work with these one at a time. First, the concept of objective measures runs against everything we know about the history of man-made things. Objectively measuring how good or bad something is requires not only that the universe is objective, but also that the people in it are objective. There is no film, book, software, website, or album that is universally liked by everyone (including those who have the word critic in their job title). Some people may be more informed or knowledgeable than others, but this doesn't make their opinions objective.

More important perhaps is measurement. Measuring how good or bad something is requires knowledge about the intent of what the thing is trying to do. If you show me a frying pan that you've made, and I criticize it for not playing MP3 files, there's a mismatch of intention in what we're trying to measure and evaluate. Unless the intention of the work is clear to everyone ("I want to make omelets"), good criticism is impossible. There are an infinite number of intentions and goals in the universe, and if two people can't agree on what the creator's intentions are, real communication is impossible. It might be fair to say that the intentions of a work should be transparent in the work itself: a toaster oven should look vaguely like something that can receive slices of bread. But where the intentions aren't clear, critics have a choice: they can trust the creator and invest more energy trying to sort out what the intentions are, or they can assume the worst about those intentions and begin criticizing what they don't understand.

Second, believing that one person has sole possession of good perspective is a contradiction in terms. Good perspective by definition means being able to recognize many valuable points of view on any matter. Two smart people might both love the latest sports-car or the new sci-fi film, but for entirely different and non-overlapping reasons. Good criticism generally comes with some degree of humility and respect for other equally valid points of view. The better the critic, the more holistic their sense of how their own perspectives and tastes fit into the diverse pool of informed opinion.

Third, respect and ridicule don't mix well. Offering good criticism is an act of respect: it is communication with the intent of helping others do better work, or understand their work better. If you are shaping sentences and remarks to be snide, snarky, or sarcastic, you're not being helpful (unless you know the recipient well enough to be comfortable teasing them about their work). It's entirely possible to offer criticism, commentary, and advice without attaching negative energy: it's just we rarely see it done properly that most of us don't realize it's possible, much less more effective.

Lastly, a valid criticism doesn't mean that the work can be fixed or is worth fixing. In many situations, responding to one kind of criticism will just make the design or the work vulnerable to another kind of criticism. A film or essay that is dark and brooding could be made lighter and funnier, but then another critic could say "it wasn't dark and brooding enough." And in some cases, fixing a particular problem will cause other problems that are worse. Until the creator explores the alternatives presented by feedback, it's impossible to know whether responding to criticism is possible, much less desirable.

Collectively, this means that criticizing and giving feedback should be a thoughtful activity. If you're flippant, arrogant, dismissive, curt or annoyed while giving feedback, you're probably making one of the four assumptions above and not giving very good criticism.

How to give critical feedback

The verb criticize, once a neutral word somewhere between praise and censure, is now mainly used in a negative sense. To say "he criticized me for being so friendly" generally means something different and less positive than "he made me think about the possible effects of being so friendly."

crit•i•cal (adj.)

1. Inclined to judge severely and find fault.

2. Characterized by careful, exact evaluation and judgment: a critical reading.

Now I'm not saying that finding fault isn't useful. On the contrary, it's very important. It's just that of equal importance in understanding the value of a design, algorithm, script, or film is to know what isn't broken, or god forbid, what's actually been done brilliantly. What you want to do when you offer criticism is to live up to the second definition listed above: careful evaluation and judgment. To achieve this you need to do the following:

1. **Before you speak, know the goals.** What problem is the work trying to solve? What are the goals? If you don't know the work's intent, it's very difficult to offer careful evaluation and judgment. Remember the frying pan? If I don't know what the creator is trying to achieve, how can I possibly offer any valuable commentary? Now it should be the creator's job to inform me of what they're trying to do, or tell me that they think it should be self-evident in the work, but if they don't, there's not much harm in me asking "what are you trying to accomplish here?" to save everyone time and grief. If the problem

is at the level of intention, discussion will ensue at that
level instead of trying (and failing) to sort out intentions
at the level of specific design choices.

2. **Good and bad, is not the same as what you like or
   don't like.** You must shatter the idea that anything
   you like is good, and anything you don't like is bad.
   If you can't separate your personal preferences from
   more abstract analysis, then you will rarely provide
   much useful feedback. Criticism is not about you. It's
   about the work you are viewing and the person who
   made it. Your personal preferences only get in the
   way of providing the work (and its maker or possible
   consumers) with useful information. Learn to see the
   good and respectable attributes in work you do not like:
   they are there if you let yourself see them. For example:
   a good film review should evaluate the film's merits
   somewhat independently from the reviewer's personal
   tastes. It should be possible to read a review about a film
   the critic didn't like, but be inclined to see it anyway
   based on the observations he made about its content,
   style, and form.

3. **Talk as much about what it is, as what it isn't.** While it
   can be more efficient to focus on problems and what's
   broken, rather than what's good and working, if the
   creator can't see both, there's not much hope that their
   next choices will be good ones. Make sure you spend as
   much energy helping them to see and keep the strong
   parts of what they've done as you do helping them to
   see the weaker and more questionable parts.

4. **Try the PNP sandwich (positive negative positive):** I
   don't like this idea much, but I think it can be a good
   one (see what I did there?) for dealing with people who
   are sensitive receiving criticism. The idea is simple:
   alternate your feedback. Say something positive, then

say something negative, then say another positive thing. It's an easy way to develop trust and help people become comfortable with hearing other people's opinion. I don't like it because it can feel forced and contrived. However I have seen it work as a way to get strangers to warm up to each other, and eventually grow out of this pattern of behavior.

Receiving critical feedback

It's much harder to receive criticism than to give it. By the time most people make it through college they have had many bad experiences with receiving feedback, especially on creative work, that they avoid it. Nothing can be worse: feedback is essential to developing ideas, and if the project involves a team in any way, the dialog and communication that falls out of feedback is essential. Anyone who makes something must find ways to not only obtain feedback, but to master the skills of milking it for all it's worth.

1. **Shut up. Just shut up and listen.** Creators often fall into the trap of speaking for their work, trying to use words to defend things that should be in the design. This is a form of denial: the work has to speak for itself. Even if only for a few minutes, let the prototype or draft be its own thing, and stand on its own. If you respond right away to (or perhaps interrupt) every point made in a critique, you can't possibly be thinking about what's being said to you. Thinking takes time. Try to talk as little as possible, and let the time be used for critique, not for defense. If you don't trust the people critiquing you to be fair, that's a problem best solved by defining sound ground rules (see below), or by investing more in finding better critique partners.

2. **Ask clarifying questions.** Again, avoid filling the conversation with defensive chatter. Instead respond to

questions by trying to sort out any ambiguities or points you don't agree with by getting whoever is critiquing to restate their point. "When you say the style in my design is sloppy, do you mean that the lines aren't sharp, or that the composition isn't balanced quite right? Can you show me exactly what you mean?" By asking clarifying questions you allow yourself time to decide if you agree with the criticism or not. It makes the critique into a dialog, which is what it should be, and not a courtroom trial.

3. **Refer back to the goals.** If you're not getting what you want from the critique, provide some goals for the work that you're trying to achieve. If you're working on a project this should be easy: the goals for a given design should derive from the project goals. Ask whoever is giving you feedback to do so in terms of those goals or your derivations of them. Then whenever the conversation goes astray, you can refer back to the goals and set things in a useful direction again.

4. **Ask for changes you can make that will satisfy the criticism.** The goal of criticism is not to learn every nuance about a design's weaknesses: it's to know enough about a design so that the designer can make it better. If you agree with a criticism, but don't see a path to improvement, ask for one. Turn the question back around on the person who made the comment. "Good point. So do you see anything I can do to improve on that?" Often they won't have anything to say: critiquing is not the same as creating. But by asking the question, you move the conversation forward into thinking about future action, instead of staying stuck in criticism mode.

Ground rules

1. **Take control of your feedback process.** Feedback is not

something that happens to you: it should be something you make happen. If you wait for feedback to come to you, it tends to be less positive and supportive than if you seek it out. If you walk into someone's office and say "hey, can I have five minutes of your time to look at something?" you are taking control. You put yourself in the driver's seat, and can frame and shape the criticism you get however you want. But if you wait and wait and wait until deadlines approach, you have less and less control over how feedback will be given to you. It will have more edge to it and will tend to serve others more than serving you.

2. **Pick your partners. Who do you get the best feedback from?** It's probably not the person who loves everything you do. If you don't think you get good feedback from anyone, part of the problem might be that you haven't taken control of the process. Be more specific about what kinds of criticism you need, and go to people and ask for it. If you find a good source, cherish it, and reward them for it. Much of what a good mentor does is provide good, consistent, honest feedback. If you can get this from a peer or a manager find ways to cultivate and reward it. Look for people outside of your company or organization who might be willing to form a peer review group: meet once a week/month over coffee and show each other your work.

3. **Strive to hear it all, informally and early.** The sooner you hear a question or criticism of something you've created, the greater your ability to do something about it before it's finished. If there is any kind of formal review or feedback process (e.g., a spec review or group critique) make it your job to find out what the opinions are about what you're doing. This can be as simple as going to door to door and showing sketches, and asking for a few quick comments. Give yourself the opportunity to

benefit early from other perspectives and think things through. But do know how much feedback you can handle: you don't want your work driven by everyone's opinions, but you do want to let good insights from others influence what you make.

HOW TO LEARN FROM YOUR MISTAKES

You can only learn from a mistake after you admit you've made it. As soon as you start blaming other people, or the universe itself, you distance yourself from any possible lesson. But if you courageously stand up and honestly say "this is my mistake and I am responsible", the possibilities for learning move toward you. Admitting a mistake, even if only privately to yourself, makes learning possible. It moves the focus away from assigning blame and toward understanding. Wise people admit their mistakes easily. They know progress accelerates when they do.

This advice runs counter to the cultural assumptions we have about mistakes and failure, namely that they are shameful things. We're taught in school, at home, and at work to feel guilty about failure and to do whatever we can to avoid mistakes. This sense of shame, combined with inevitable setbacks when attempting difficult things explains why many people give up on their goals: they're not prepared for the mistakes and failures they'll face along the way. What's missing in many people's beliefs about success is the fact that the more challenging the goal, the more frequent and difficult setbacks will be. The larger your ambitions, the more dependent you will be on your ability to overcome and learn from your mistakes.

In many cultures our work represents us: if you fail a test, you are a failure. If you make a mistake, you are a mistake. It's telling that letter grades (A,B,C,D, F) are given both to students and to things we eat. It's a way to accelerate sorting through large quantities of something. Grades allow universities and corporations to make judgments based on tests that are unforgiving to mistakes and ignorant of talents that can not be easily measured.

For anyone without a strong sense of self, based not on lack of mistakes but on courage, compassionate intelligence, commitment, and creativity, life is a scary place. It's easiest to play it safe by never getting into trouble, never breaking rules, and never taking the risks that their hearts tell them they need to take.

Learning from mistakes requires three things:

1. Putting yourself in situations where you can make interesting mistakes.

2. Having the self-confidence to admit to them.

3. Being courageous about making changes.

This essay will cover all three. First we have to classify the different kinds of mistakes.

The four kinds of mistakes

One way to categorize mistakes is into these categories[3]:

1. **Stupid:** dumb things that just happen. Stubbing your toe, dropping your pizza on your neighbor's fat cat or poking yourself in the eye with a banana.

2. **Simple:** Mistakes that are avoidable but your sequence of decisions made inevitable. Having the power go out in the middle of your party because you forgot to pay the rent, or running out of beer at said party because you didn't anticipate the number of guests.

3. **Involved:** Mistakes that are understood but require effort to prevent. Regularly arriving late to work, eating fast food for lunch every day, or going bankrupt at your start-up company because of your complete ignorance of basic accounting.

4. **Complex:** Mistakes that have complicated causes with no obvious way to avoid them next time. Examples include marriages that fail, tough decisions that have bad results either way you go, or other unpleasant or unsatisfying outcomes to important things you invested energy in but didn't work out anyway.

Learning from mistakes that fall into the first two categories (Stupid & Simple) is easy, but shallow. Once you recognize the problem and know the better way, you should be able to avoid similar mistakes. Or in some cases you'll realize that no matter what you do, once in a while, you'll still do stupid things (e.g., even Einstein stubbed his toes).

---

[3] I'm sure you have ideas for other categories: that's fantastic. But these are the ones you're stuck with for the rest of this essay. I'm also leaving philosophical questions about mistakes up to you. One person's pleasure is another person's mistake: decide for yourself. Maybe you enjoy stabbing your neighbor's cat with a banana, who knows. We all do things we know are bad in the long term, but are oh so good in the short term. However mistakes are defined in your personal philosophy, this essay should help you learn from them.

But these kinds of mistakes are not interesting. The lessons aren't deep and it's unlikely they lead you to learn much about yourself or anything else. For example, compare these two mistakes:

1. My use of dual part harmony for the second trumpets in my orchestral composition for the homeless children's shelter benefit concert overpowered the intended narrative of the violins.

2. I got an Oreo stuck in my underwear.

The kind of mistakes you make define you. The more interesting the mistakes, the more interesting the life. If your biggest mistakes are missing tv-show reruns or buying the wrong lottery ticket, you're not challenging yourself enough to earn more interesting mistakes.

And since there isn't much to learn from simple and stupid mistakes, most people try to minimize their frequency and how much time they spend recovering from them. Their time is better spent learning from bigger mistakes. But if we habitually or compulsively make stupid mistakes, what we really have is an involved mistake.

Involved mistakes

This third pile of mistakes, Involved mistakes, requires significant change to avoid. These are mistakes we tend to make through either habit or nature. But since change is so much harder than we admit, we often suffer through the same mistakes again and again rather than making the tough changes needed to avoid them.

Difficultly with change involves an earlier point made in this essay. Some feel that to agree to change means there is something wrong with them. "If I'm perfect, why would I need to change?" Since they need to protect their idea of perfection, they refuse change. Or possibly, even refuse to admit they did anything wrong.

But this is a trap. Refusal to acknowledge mistakes, or tendencies to make similar kinds of mistakes, is a denial of reality. If you can't see the gaps, flaws, or weaknesses in your behavior you're forever trapped in the same behavior and limitations you've always had, possibly since you were a child. When someone tells you you're being a baby, they might be right.

Another challenge to change is that it may require renewing commitments you've broken before, from the trivial "Yes, I'll try to remember to take the trash out," to the more serious "I'll try to stop sleeping with all of your friends." This happens in any environment: the workplace, friendships, romantic relationships or even commitments you've made to yourself. Renewing commitments can be tough because it requires not only admitting to the recent mistake, but acknowledging similar mistakes you've made before. The feelings of failure and guilt become so large that we don't have the courage to try again.

This is why successfully learning from mistakes often requires other people, either for advice, training, or simply to keep you honest. A supportive friend's, mentor's or professional's perspective on your behavior will be more objective than your own and help you identify when you're breaking the commitments you've made. In moments of weakness the only way to prevent a mistake is to enlist someone else. "Fred, I want to play my Xbox today but I promised Sally I wouldn't. Can we hang out so you can make sure I don't play it today?" Admitting you need help and asking for it often requires more courage than trying to do it on your own.

The biggest lesson in involved mistakes is that you have to

examine your own ability to change. Some kinds of change will be easier for you than others and until you make mistakes and try to correct them you won't know which they are.

How to handle complex mistakes

The most interesting kinds of mistake are complex mistakes. The more complicated the mistake you've made, the more patient you need to be. There's nothing worse than flailing around trying to fix something you don't understand: you'll always make things worse.

I remember as a kid when our beloved Atari 2600 game system started showing static on the screen during games. The solution my brother and I came up with? Smack the machine as hard as we could (a clear sign I had the intellect for management.) Amazingly this worked for awhile, but after weeks of regular beatings, the delicate electronics eventually gave out. We were lazy, ignorant, and impatient, and couldn't see that our solution would work against us.

Professional investigators, like journalists, police detectives and doctors, try to get as many perspectives on situations as possible before taking action. Policemen use eyewitnesses, doctors use exams and tests, scientific studies use large sample sizes. They know that human perception, including their own, is highly fallible and biased by many factors. The only way to obtain an objective understanding is to compare several different perspectives. When trying to understand your own mistakes in complex situations you should work in the same way.

Start by finding someone else to talk to about what happened. Even if no one was within 50 yards when you crashed your best friend's BMW into your neighbor's living room, talking to someone else gives you the benefit of applying their experience to your situation. They may know of someone who's made a similar mistake or have an idea for dealing with the problem that you don't.

Most importantly, by describing what happened you are forced to break down the chronology and clearly define your recollection of the sequence of events. They may ask you questions that surface important details you didn't notice before. There may have been more going on (Did the brakes fail? Did you swerve to avoid your neighbor's daughter?) than you, consumed by your emotions about your failure, realized.

If multiple people were involved you want to hear each person's account of what happened. Each person will emphasize different aspects of the situation based on their skills, biases, and circumstances, getting you closer to a complete view of what took place.

If the situation was contentious you may need people to report their stories independently – police investigators never have eyewitnesses collaborate. They want each point of view to be delivered unbiased by other eyewitnesses' possibly erroneous recollections. Later on they'll bring each account together and see what fits and what doesn't.

An illustrative example comes from James R. Chiles' book *Inviting Disaster: Lessons from the Edge of Technology*. It tells the story of a floating dormitory for oil workers in the North Sea that rolled over during the night killing more than 100 people. The engineering experts quickly constructed different theories and complex explanations that focused on operational errors and management decisions.

All of these theories were wrong. It was eventually discovered through careful analysis that weeks earlier, a crack in a support structure had been painted over, instead of being reported and repaired. This stupid, simple, and small mistake caused the superstructure to fail, sinking the dormitory. Without careful analysis, the wrong conclusion would have been reached (e.g., smacking the Atari) and the wrong lesson would have been learned.

Until you work backwards from the moments, hours or days before the actual mistake occured, you probably won't see all of the contributing factors and can't learn all of the possible lessons. The more complex the mistake, the further back you'll need to go and the more careful and open-minded you need to be in your own investigation. You may even need to bring in an objective outsider to help sort things out. You'd never have a suspect in a crime lead the investigation, right? So how can you completely trust yourself to investigate your own mistakes?

Here are some questions to help your investigation:

1. What was the probable sequence of events?

2. Did multiple small mistakes lead to a larger one?

3. Were any erroneous assumptions made?

4. Did we have the right goals? Were we trying to solve the right problem?

5. Was it possible to have recognized bad assumptions earlier?

6. Was there information we know now that would have been useful then?

7. What would we do differently if in this exact situation again?

8. How can we avoid getting into situations like this? (What was the kind of situation we wanted to be in?)

9. Was this simply unavoidable given all of the circumstances? A failure isn't a mistake if you were attempting the impossible.

10. Has enough time passed for us to know if this is a mistake or not?

As you put together the sequence of events, you'll recognize that mistakes initially categorized as complex eventually break down into smaller mistakes. The painted-over crack was avoidable but happened anyway (Stupid). Was there a system in place for avoiding these mistakes? (Simple). Were there unaddressed patterns of behavior that made that system fail? (Involved). Once you've deconstructed a complex mistake, you can follow the previous advice on making changes.

Humor and courage

No amount of analysis can replace your confidence in yourself. When you've made a mistake, especially a visible one that impacts other people, it's natural to question your ability to perform next time. But you must get past your doubts. The best you can do is study the past, practice for the situations you expect, and get back in the game. Studying the past should help broaden your perspective. Be aware of how many other smart, capable, well-meaning people have made similar mistakes to the one you made, yet still had even bigger mistakes, I mean successes, in the future.

One way to know you've reached a healthy place is your sense of humor. It might take a few days, but eventually you'll see some comedy in what happened. When friends tell stories of their mistakes it makes you laugh, right? Well when you can laugh at your mistake, you know you've accepted it and no longer judge yourself on the basis of one single event. Reaching this kind of perspective is very important in avoiding future mistakes. Humor loosens up your psychology and prevents you from obsessing about the past. It's easy to make new mistakes by spending too much energy protecting against the previous ones. Remember the saying "a man fears the tiger that bit him last, instead of the tiger that will bite him next."

So the most important lesson in all of mistake making is to trust that while mistakes are inevitable, if you can learn from the current one, you'll also be able to learn from future ones. No matter what happens tomorrow, you'll be able to get value from it, and apply it to the day after that. Progress won't be a straight line but if you keep learning you will have more successes than failures, and the mistakes you make along the way will help you get to where you want to go.

Here is the learning from mistakes checklist:

1. Accepting responsibility makes learning possible.

2. Don't equate making mistakes with being a mistake.

3. You can't change mistakes, but you can choose how you respond to them.

4. Growth starts when you can see room for improvement.

5. Work to understand why it happened and what the factors were.

6. What information could have avoided the mistake?

7. What small mistakes, in sequence, contributed to the bigger mistake?

8. Are there alternatives you should have considered but did not?

9. What kinds of changes are required to avoid making

this mistake again? What kinds of change are difficult for you?

10. How do you think your behavior should/would change if you were in a similar situation again?

11. Work to understand the mistake until you can make fun of it (or not want to kill others that make fun).

12. Keep your perspective: the next situation won't be the same as the last. Your next mistake might be the result of your response to the last mistake, if you focus too much on what happened, instead of what is likely to happen in the future.

HOW TO KEEP YOUR MOUTH SHUT

I have the disease known as "cannot keep mouth shut." If I think someone is wrong, my arm raises, and my mouth engages, well before my brain can calculate the possible damage. I have been in recovery for years and am here to share what I've learned.

As a rule, if you insist on speaking your mind, you will inevitably find yourself somewhere where everyone hates you. Most people cannot handle the truth. And the more you shove it in their face, the easier it is for them to ignore you. You simply become the person who always complains, rendering any good ideas you have entirely impotent. Your ideas will be shot down simply because of the reputation of the mouth they come from.

The trick to keeping your mouth shut is to hold the desire to create change above your desire to tell people how wrong and bad they are. The latter almost never leads to the former.

In my early career I worked on strong teams where you were expected to have opinions. If you saw something stupid happening, you were obligated to raise your hand and say "I think this is stupid and here's why." If you were right, you were applauded no matter how senior the people in the room were. I argued with group managers, VPs, and other scary, tough, smart people, and in the culture this was fine, provided I had a point. If I was wrong, I'd be dismissed, but not roasted. I might even have gotten mild praise for not being afraid. I thrived in this environment and assumed this was how the world worked.

But later on, in a different organization, I discovered a world of dysfunction, despair, and passive aggression. No one spoke their mind. Few worked hard or asked tough questions. Quality of work, and morale, was low. I felt obligated to mention these facts as often and as loudly as possible to leadership. I even expected to be rewarded for telling people how bad things were. Why wouldn't they want to hear this? I thought.

Within a month, I was that guy. The guy who always complains. I expected to be applauded for pointing out failure. It was a leadership act in my mind and past experience. But I didn't consider that this group had its own standards and its own way of dealing with things below those standards. After months of misery I realized something I should have known from the beginning: I was in a different culture with different expectations. Sounds idiotic now, but I was too immature to know the rest of the world was not like the small part of the world I came from.

I realized in past jobs progress happened not simply because I was right and spoke my mind, as much as my ego wished this to be true. Progress happened because my boss, or his/her boss, listened to my points and took action, or granted me the power to do so. Having an idea changes nothing unless someone with sufficient power does something about it. The idea alone is never enough, nor is saying it out loud. No matter how loud you yell, talking and doing are not the same thing.

In the movie *Glengarry Glenn Ross*, Blake (played by Alec Baldwin) gives the meanest most degrading lecture of all time to some struggling salesmen. Why is this lecture possible? Why didn't they ignore him or beat him up? Is it young Alec's strong chin and trim physique? No, it's because the owners of the company asked him to do it. He's allowed to open his mouth, and speak a certain kind of truth, however unnecessarily mean and adversarial, because he has the support of those in power. When in doubt, look up. Those with the big salaries define the playing field and the rules of engagement.

Later in the same movie, a salesman (played by Al Pacino) yells at the sales manager (played by Kevin Spacey), for ruining a deal by speaking too much. He tells him "You never open your mouth until you know what the shot is". This is a great rule to follow before you raise objections or offer big ideas. No matter how right you are, if you care about effecting change, never open your mouth without knowing who will agree with you and who won't. If you can anticipate the angles and responses, and judge, even by guessing, if there is an 80%, 20%, or 0% chance anyone in good standing will follow your lead in support of what you say, you know whether it's worth speaking up. There's a world of difference in having your point met only with silence, versus someone respected saying "he might be right".

There are times when problems are so bad you have to speak the truth no matter the consequences. But pick your battles. If a year goes by and you haven't taken a single stand, I'd call you a coward. You must draw your sword now and then to remind people you have one. But if you're taking a stand every day, you're a glutton for punishment, an egomaniac, or too stupid to realize you're working for the wrong people.

CREATIVE THINKING HACKS

Each one of us possesses everything necessary to be more creative. The problem is that schools, parents, and workplaces tend to reward us for following rules. It's something quite different to learn to ask our own questions and seek our own answers (which is one simple definition of creative thinking). This essay is a high-speed, condensed version of a course I taught at the University of Washington on how anyone, with some honest effort, can easily become more creative at any task at any time.

Kill creative romance

Like most media today, this essay starts with violence—and an unnecessary exclamation point! Close your eyes, and imagine the most amazing sword ever made. Now, with it in hand, attack every creative legend you've ever heard. (We've romanticized da Vinci, Mozart, and Einstein into gods, minimizing the ordinary aspects of their lives so intensely that their mothers wouldn't recognize them in the legends we tell.) Next, using your sword's mint-scented flamethrower attachment, set fire to childhood tales of Isaac Newton and the apple, Benjamin Franklin and the lightning kite, and Edison and the lightbulb. Think of other similar legends you've heard, even if they were not mentioned in *The Myths of Innovation*. These popular tales of creativity are deceptive at best, wild lies at worst. They're shaped to placate the masses, not to inform or help people actually interested in doing creative work. Slash each and every one with your sword, throw a dozen napalm-coated hand grenades in for good measure, and watch your old, broken-down view of creativity go up in flames. Dance around the smoldering ruins! Roast marshmallows over the still-warm remains of your creative fulminations! The fun begins now: free yourself. Feel like you did when you were young, without any preconceptions over what is or is not creative.

In this new landscape, plant the following simple definition: an idea is a combination of other ideas. Say it five times out loud. Say it to your cat. Yell it out your car window at strangers waiting for the bus. Every amazing creative thing you've ever seen or idea you've ever heard can be broken down into smaller ideas that existed before. An automobile? An engine and wheels. A telephone? Electricity and sound. Reese's Peanut Butter Cups? Peanut butter and chocolate. All great creative ideas, inventions, and theories are composed of other ideas. Why should you care? Because if you want to be a creator instead of a consumer, you must view existing ideas as fuel for your mind. You must stop seeing them as objects or functional things—they are combinations of ingredients waiting to be reused.

Combinations

Cooking is a brilliant analogy for creativity: a chef's talents hinge on his ability to bring ingredients together to create things. Even the most inspired chef in history did not make bacon appear by mere concentration, nor suggest to the divine forces that a ripe tomato should be on the list of evolution's desired outcomes. Faith in the creativity-as-combinations view of the world helps creators in many ways. It means that if at any time you feel uncreative, the solution is to look more carefully at the combinations available to you, or to break apart something to see how it's made. Increasing creativeness doesn't require anything more than increasing your observations: become more aware of possible combinations. Here's a test: quickly pick two things in front of you, say, this book and your annoying, smelly friend Rupert. Now close your eyes and imagine different ways to combine them.

If you're stuck, here are three:

1. Rupert with a table of contents

2. An annoying, smelly book about innovation

3. Reading a book on, or making one out of, Rupert's face

Now while these combos might not be useful, good, or even practical, they're certainly creative (and if you think these are stupid and juvenile, you have confused bad taste with lack of creativity). Adding a third element, perhaps a gallon of cappuccino, might yield even more interesting combinations (a caffeine-overdosed, smelly book infused with Rupert's annoying personality).

Over time, creative masters learn to find, evaluate, and explore more combinations than other people. They get better at guessing which combinations will be more interesting, so their odds improve. They also learn there are reusable patterns that can be used to develop new ideas. For example, musicians throughout history have reused melodies, chord progressions, and even entire song structures. The national anthem of the United States was based on the tune of an old British drinking song[4]. The Disney film *The Lion King* is a retelling of Shakespeare's *Hamlet*. Shakespeare was likely influenced by the

---

[4] http://en.wikipedia.org/wiki/The_Star-Spangled_Banner.

early Greek tragedies. Study any creative field, from comedy to cooking to writing, and you'll discover patterns of reuse and recombination everywhere. It's an illusion that when an artist makes a painting or an author writes a novel it appeared magically into her hands from out of nowhere. Everything comes from somewhere, no matter how amazing or wonderful the thing is. The *Mona Lisa* was not the first portrait any more than the Destiny's Child song "Survivor" was the first four-minute R&B hit.

I'm not suggesting you steal something someone else made and put your name on it. That's theft, and a fairly uncreative kind of theft at that. Instead, the goal is to recognize how much in the world there is to borrow from, reuse, reinterpret, use as inspiration, or recombine without breaking laws or violating trust. Every field has its own rules and limitations, but creative fields are more liberal than you'd expect[5].

Inhibition

We're afraid. We're afraid of the dark, of our parents, and of what our parents do in the dark. Our tiny, efficient brains do their best to keep us from thinking about things we fear or don't understand. This is good for survival but bad for combination making. We shut down the pursuit of many combinations because of predictions we make about what the result will be. But remember: we suck at prediction. Lewis Thomas mentioned the best sign of progress in his research lab was laughter, and laughter often comes from surprise.

Many of us who have the potential to be creative fail only because we struggle to turn off our filters and fears. We don't want to do anything that could yield an unexpected result.

---

[5] An interesting challenge to this claim is the issue of sampling in music. How much of one song can another artist sample and reuse? One second? Five? None? See the excellent film *Copyright Criminals*, which explores this question from many different perspectives (and there's lots of good music in the film, too): http://www.pbs.org/independentlens/copyright-criminals/film.html.

We seek external validation from our teachers, bosses, family, etc., but creativity usually depends on internal validation. We have to judge for ourselves whether our ideas are interesting or useful.

One way to think of creative people is that they have more control over their fears—or less fear of embarrassment. They're not necessarily smarter or more capable of coming up with good ideas, they simply filter out fewer ideas than the rest of us. Creativity has more to do with being fearless than intelligent or any other adjective superficially associated with it. This explains why many people feel more creative when drinking, using drugs, or late at night: these are all times when their inhibitions are lower, or at least altered, and they allow themselves to see more combinations of things than they do normally.

Environment

Creativity is personal. No book or expert can dictate how you can be more creative. You have to spend time paying attention to yourself: when do ideas come easiest to you? Are you alone? With friends? In a bar? At the beach? Are there times of day when you're most relaxed? Is there music playing? Start paying attention to your rhythms and then construct your creative activities around them. To get all Emersonian on you, this is called self-knowledge. You can't be productive as a creator if you're not paying attention to your own behavior and cultivating the unique wonder in this universe that is you . Nothing is more counterintuitive than trying to be yourself by being like other people. It doesn't work that way—no book, course, or teacher can give this to you.

To help you figure this out, you need to experience different ways of working, and pay attention to which ones best suit you. They might be unexpected, not fitting into your framework (i.e., filters) for how creative work should be done, or what's appropriate for a 42-year-old middle manager to do. I learned that I tend to be most creative late at night. I don't find it convenient, and neither does my family, but I've recognized it to be true. If I want to maximize my creativity, I will spend hours working late at night. Each of us responds to environmental conditions differently. Half the challenge is experimenting to find out which ones work best; the other half is honoring them despite how inconvenient or unexpected they might be.

Persistence

Being creative for kicks is easy. But if you want to be creative on demand you must develop helpful habits, and that's about persistence. You won't always find interesting combinations for a problem right away, and identifying fears and working through them is rarely fun. At some point, all creative tasks become work. The interesting and fun challenges fade, and the ordinary, boring, inglorious work necessary to bring an idea to the world becomes the reality. Study the histories of great creators, and you'll find a common core of willpower and commitment as their driving force. Van Gogh, Michelangelo, and Mozart worked every day. Edison, Hemingway, and Beethoven, as well as most legendary talents, outworked their peers. Forget brilliance or genetics, the biggest difference between the greats and us was their dedication to their craft. Each of the names we know had peers who were just as talented, or more so, but twice as lazy. They consistently gave up before their projects were finished. Want to guess why we don't know their names? The world can only care about ideas that are shared.

When I give lectures on creative thinking, I often ask who in the audience has had an idea for a business, movie, or book. Most of the audience raises their hands. I then ask how many people have done any work at all on these ideas, and most of the audience drops their hands. That tells the whole story: ideas are lazy. They don't do anything on their own. If you aren't willing to do the ordinary work to make the idea real, the problem isn't about creativity at all.

When an idea is fully formed in your head, there's no escaping the fact that for the idea to change the world, it has to leave your brain—a journey that only happens with hard work and dedication. Writing proposals, sketching designs, pitching ideas: it's all work you know how to do. But how far are you actually willing to go to make your idea real?

Creative thinking hacks

Here are some clever tactics for applying this advice:

- **Start an idea journal.** Write down any idea that pops in your mind at any time. Don't be inhibited: anything goes. You will never have to show anyone else this journal, so there should be no filters—it's safe from judgment. This should help you find your own creative rhythms, as over time you can note what times of day you're more creative. I recommend a paper journal so you can doodle and write freely, but digital journals also work. Whenever you're stuck, flip through your journal. You're bound to find an old idea you've forgotten about that can be used toward the problem you're trying to solve.

- **Give your subconscious a chance.** The reason ideas come to you in the shower is that you're relaxed enough for your subconscious to surface ideas. Make this easier: find time to turn your mind off. Run, swim, bike, have sex, do something that's as far from your creative problem as possible. Afterward, you might just find that the problem you struggled with all morning isn't as hard, or that you have a new idea for approaching it.

- **Use your body to help your mind.** This is entirely counter- intuitive to your logical mind, but that's exactly why it's so likely to work. In John Medina's *Brain Rules*, he explains how physical activity, even for people who don't like it, has positive effects on brain function. The theory is that for most of our evolutionary history, the acts of physical exertion and maximum brain function were correlated (think how creative you have to be when being chased by tigers). If your body is active, your mind will follow. Einstein and Bohr used to debate physics while going for long walks—they both believed they thought better when moving around. This might be true for you.

- **Inversion.** If you're stuck, come up with ideas for the opposite of what you want. If your goal was to design the best website for your team, switch to designing the worst one you can imagine. Five minutes at an inverted problem will get your frustrations out, make you laugh, and likely get you past your fears. Odds are high you'll hit something so horribly bad that it's interesting, and in studying it, you'll discover good ideas you would never have found any other way.

- **Switch modes.** Everyone has a dominant way of expressing ideas: sketching, writing, talking. If you switch the mode you're working in, different ideas are easier to find, and your understanding of a particular problem will change. This is both a way to find new ideas and to explore an idea you're focused on. Working on paper, rather than computers, can make this easier because you can doodle in the margins (a form of mode switching), something you can't really do with a mouse and a keyboard. Or, try explaining your problem to a child, or to the smartest person you know, which will force you to describe and think about the problem differently.

- **Take an improvisational comedy class.** This will be

easier and less painful than you think. These classes, offered for ordinary people by most improv comedy groups, are structured around simple games. You show up, play some games, and slowly each week you learn how to pay more attention to the situations the games put you in, as well as how to respond to them. You will eventually become more comfortable with investing in combinations without being sure of the outcome.

- **Find a partner.** Some people are most creative when they're with creative friends. Partnering up on a project, or even being around other creative people who are working on solo projects, keeps energy levels high. They will bring a new perspective to your ideas, and you will bring a new perspective to theirs. It also gives you a drinking buddy when things go sour.

- **Stop reading and start doing.** The word create is a verb. Be active. Go make things. Make dinner, make a drawing, make a fire, make some noise, but make. If all your attempts at being creative consist of passively consuming, no matter how brilliant what you consume is, you'll always be a consumer, not a creator. An entire culture of tinkerers and makers is out there, with projects and tools to help you get started. Check out makezine.com and www.readymade.com, two sites waiting to show you the way.

DR. SEUSS, WICKED CONSTRAINTS AND CREATIVE THINKING

There's good evidence we get creative fuel from constraints. Dr. Seuss, the author of *The Cat in The Hat*, and many books that followed, met a requirement to use only 250 different words.

In May 1954, *Life* magazine published a report on literacy among school children, which concluded that children were not learning to read because their books were boring. Accordingly, Dr. Theodor Seuss Geisel's publisher made up a list of 348 words he felt were important and asked Geisel [a.k.a Dr. Seuss] to cut the list to 250 words and write a book using only those words. Nine months later, Geisel, using 236 of the words given to him, completed The Cat in the Hat. This book was a tour de force – it retained the drawing style, verse rhythms, and all the imaginative power of Geisel's earlier works, but because of its simplified vocabulary, beginners could read it. These books achieved significant international success and remain very popular.

Of course this isn't to say that all constraints are good. Some constraints make a solution impossible. If I asked you to build me a spaceship to Saturn by noon tomorrow that cost $5.50, it would be insane to blame your failure to solve the problem on lack of creativity. But on the other hand, President John F. Kennedy's proclamation to go put a man on the moon by 1970 seemed impossible to many when he said it in 1962.

Persistence at a poorly defined problem is futile, and talent applied to a unsolvable problem is worthless. The challenge is knowing how to define problems with enough constraints to help creativity, but not so many that creativity, or any solution, is impossible. Mastering this skill is one secret that explains who successfully makes things and who doesn't.

WHY SMART PEOPLE DEFEND BAD IDEAS

We all know someone who is intelligent, but who occasionally defends obviously bad ideas. Why does this happen? How can smart people take up positions that defy any reasonable logic? Having spent many years working with smart people I've catalogued many of the ways this happens, and I have advice on what to do about it. I feel qualified to write this essay as I'm a recovering smart person myself, and I've defended several very bad ideas. So if nothing else, this essay serves as a kind of personal therapy session where I embarrass myself for your pleasure.

Success at defending bad ideas

I'm not always proud to admit I have a degree in Logic and Computation from Carnegie Mellon University. Majoring in logic is not something that makes people want to talk to you at parties or read your essays. But one thing I learned after years of studying advanced logic theory is proficiency in argument can easily be used to overpower others, even when you are dead wrong. If you learn a few tricks of logic and debate, you can refute the obvious, and defend the ridiculous. If the people you're arguing with aren't as comfortable with argument tactics, or aren't as arrogant as you are, they may even give in and agree with you.

The problem with smart people is that they like to be right, and sometimes will defend ideas to the death rather than admit they're wrong. This is bad. Worse, if they got away with it when they were young (say, because they were smarter than their parents, their friends, and their parents' friends) they've probably built an ego around being right and will therefore defend their perfect record of invented righteousness to the death. Smart people often fall into the trap of preferring to be right even if it's based in delusion, or results in them, or their loved ones, becoming miserable. Somewhere in your town cemetery is a row of graves called smartypants lane, filled with people who were buried at poorly attended funerals, whose headstones say "Well, at least I was right."

Until these people meet someone tenacious enough to dissect their logic, and resilient enough to endure the thinly veiled intellectual abuse they dish out during debate (e.g. "You don't really think that do you?"), they're never forced to question their ability to defend bad ideas. Opportunities for this are rare: a new boss, a new co-worker, a new friend. But if their obsessive-ness about being right is strong enough, they'll reject those people out of hand, before they question their own biases and self-manipulations. Or the people they meet will quickly give up on trying to show them a better way of thinking. It can be easier for smart people who have a habit of defending bad ideas to change jobs, spouses, or cities than examine what is at the core of their psychology, and often, their misery.

Short of obtaining a degree in logic, or studying the nuances of debate, remember this one simple rule for defusing those who are skilled at defending bad ideas: simply because they cannot be proven wrong, does not make them right. Most of the tricks of logic and debate refute questions and attacks, but fail to establish any true justification for a given idea.

For example, just because you can't prove that I'm not the king of France re-incarnated doesn't make it true. So when someone tells you "My plan A is the best because no one has explained how it will fail" know that there is a logical gap in this argument. Simply because no one has described how it will fail, doesn't necessarily make it the best plan. It's possible that plans B, C, D and E all have the same quality, or that the reason no one has described how A will fail is because no one has had more than 30 seconds to scrutinize the plan. As we'll discuss later, defusing bad thinking requires someone, probably you, to construct a healthier framework around the bad thinking that shows it for what it is.

Death by homogony

The second stop on our tour of commonly defended bad ideas is the seemingly friendly notion of communal thinking. Just because everyone in the room is smart doesn't mean that collectively they will arrive at smart ideas. The power of peer pressure is that it works on our psychology, not our intellect. As social animals we are heavily influenced by how the people around us behave, and the quality of our own internal decision making varies widely depending on the environment we're in. (e.g. For example, try writing a haiku poem while standing in an elevator with 20 opera singers screaming 15 different operas, in 10 different languages, in falsetto, directly at you versus sitting on a bench in quiet park with all the time and solace you wish for).

That said, the more homogeneous a group of people are in their thinking, the narrower the range of ideas that the group will openly consider. The more open minded, creative, and courageous, a group is, the wider the pool of ideas they'll be capable of exploring.

Some teams of people look to focus groups, consultancies, and research methods to bring in outside ideas, but this rarely improves the quality of thinking in the group itself. Those outside ideas, however bold or original, are at the mercy of the diversity of thought within the group itself. If the collective group is only capable of approving B level work, it doesn't matter how many A level ideas you bring. Focus groups or other outside sources of information can not give a team, or its leaders, a soul. A bland homogeneous team of people has no real opinions, because it consists of people with same backgrounds, outlooks, and experiences who will only feel comfortable discussing the safe ideas that fit into those constraints.

If you want your smart people to be as smart as possible, seek a diversity of ideas. Find people with different experiences, opinions, backgrounds, weights, heights, races, facial hair styles, colors, pastimes, favorite items of clothing, philosophies, and beliefs. Unify them around the results you want, not the means or approaches they are expected to use. It's the only way to guarantee that the best ideas from your smartest people will be received openly by the people around them. On your own, avoid homogenous books, films, music, food, sex, media and people. Actually experience life by going to places you don't usually go, spending time with people you don't usually spend time with. Be in the moment and be open to it. Until recently in human history, life was much less predictable and were forced to encounter things not always of our own choosing. We are capable of more interesting and creative lives than our modern cultures often provide for us. If you go out of you way to find diverse experiences it will become impossible for you to miss ideas simply because your homogeneous outlook filtered them out.

Thinking at the wrong level

At any moment on any project there are an infinite number of levels of problem solving. Part of being a truly smart person is knowing which level is the right one at a given time. For example, if you are skidding out of control at 95 mph in your broken down Winnebago on an ice covered interstate, when a semi-truck filled with both poorly packaged fireworks and loosely bundled spark plugs slams on its brakes, it's not the right time to discuss with your passengers where they'd like to stop for dinner[6]. But as ridiculous as this scenario sounds, it happens all the time. People worry about the wrong thing at the wrong time and apply their intelligence in ways that doesn't serve whatever they're trying to achieve. Some call this wisdom, in that the wise know what to be thinking about, where as the merely intelligent only know how to think. (The de-emphasis of wisdom is an east vs. west dichotomy: eastern philosophy heavily emphasizes deeper wisdom, where-as the post enlightenment west, and America in particular, heavily emphasizes intelligence).

In the software industry, the common example of thinking at the wrong level is a team of rock star programmers who can make anything, but don't really know what to make. So they tend to build whatever things come to mind, never stopping to find someone who might not be adept at writing code, but can see where the value of their programming skills would be best applied. Other examples include people who always worry about money despite how much they have, people who struggle with relationships but invest their energy only in improving their appearance (instead of in therapy or other emotional exploration), or anyone that wants to solve problem X but only ever seems to do things that solve problem Y.

The primary point is that no amount of intelligence can help an individual who is diligently working at the wrong level of

[6] It turns out spark-plugs are entirely safe to have near fireworks, even in Winnebagos.

the problem. Someone with wisdom has to tap them on the shoulder and say, "Um, hey. The hole you're digging is very nice, and it is the right size. But you're in the wrong yard."

Killed in the long term by short term thinking

From what we know of evolution it's clear that we are alive because of our inherited ability to think quickly and respond to change. The survival of living creatures, for most of the history of our planet, has been a short term game. Only if you can out-run your predators, and catch your prey, do you have the luxury of worrying about tomorrow. It follows then that we tend to be better at worrying about and solving short term problems than long term issues. Even when we recognize an important long term issue that we need to plan for, say protecting natural resources or saving for retirement, we're all too easily distracted away from those deep thoughts by immediate things like dinner or sex (important things no doubt, but the driving needs in these pursuits, at least for my half of the species, are short term in nature). Once distracted, we rarely return to the long term issues we were drawn away from.

A common justification for the abuse of short term thinking is the fake perspective defense. The wise, but less confident guy says "Hey – are you sure we should be doing this?" And the smart, confident, but less wise guy says "Of course. We did this last time, and the time before that, so why shouldn't we do this again?". This is the fake perspective defense because there's no reason to believe that two points of data (ie. last time + the time before that) is sufficient to make claims about the future. People say similar things all the time in defense of the free market economy, democracy, and mating strategies. "Well, it's gotten us this far, and it's the best system we have". Well, maybe. But if you were in that broken down Winnebago up to your ankles in gasoline from a leaking tank, smoking a cigarette in each hand, you could say the same thing.

Put simply, the fact that you're not dead yet doesn't mean that the things you've done up until now shouldn't have, by all that is fair in the universe, already killed you. You might just need a few more data points for the law of averages to catch up, and put a permanent end to your short term thinking.

How many data points you need to feel comfortable continuing a behavior is entirely a matter of personal philosophy. The wise and skeptical know that even an infinite number of data points in the past may only have limited bearing on the future. You see, the problem with the future is that it's different than the past. We stink at prediction. So our data from the past, no matter how big a pile of data it is, may very well be entirely irrelevant. Some find this lack of predictive ability of the future quite frustrating, while others see it as the primary reason to stick around for a few more years.

Anyway, my point is not that Winnebagos or free market economies are bad. Instead I'm saying that short term bits of data are neither reliable nor a wise way to go about making important long term decisions. Intelligent people do this all the time, and since it's so commonly accepted as a rule of thumb (last time + the time before that), it's often accepted in place of actual thinking.. Always remember that humans, given our evolution, are very bad at seeing the cumulative effects of behavior. We underestimate how things like compound interest or that one cigarette a day, can in the long term, have surprisingly large impacts despite clearly small term effects.

How to prevent smart people from defending bad ideas

I spent my freshman year at a small college in New Jersey called Drew University. I had a fun time, ingested many tasty alcoholic beverages, and went to lots of great parties (the result of course was I failed out and had to move back to Queens with my parents. You see, the truth is this essay is really a public service announcement paid for by my parents - I was a smart kid that did some stupid things). But the reason I mention all this is because I learned a great bit of philosophy from many hours of playing pool in the college student center. The lesson is this: **speed kills**. I was never very good at pool, but this one guy there was, and whenever we'd play, he'd watch me miss easy shots because I tried to force them in with authority. I chose speed and power over control, and I usually lost. So, like pool, when it comes to defusing smart people who are defending bad ideas, you have to find ways to slow things down.

The reason for this is simple. Smart people, or at least those whose brains have good first gears, use their speed in thought to overpower others. They'll jump between assumptions quickly, throwing out jargon, bits of logic, or rules of thumb at a rate of fire fast enough to cause most people to become rattled, and give in. When that doesn't work, the arrogant or the pompous will throw in some belittlement and use whatever snide or manipulative tactics they have at their disposal to further discourage you from dissecting their ideas.

Your best defense starts by breaking an argument down into pieces. When someone says "it's obvious we need to execute plan A now." You say, "hold on. You're way ahead of me. For me to follow I need to break this down into pieces." And without waiting for permission, you should go ahead and do so.

First, nothing is obvious. If it were obvious there would be no need to say so. So your first piece is to establish what isn't so obvious. What are the assumptions the other guy is glossing over that are worth spending time on? There may be three or four valid assumptions that need to be discussed one at a time before decisions can be considered. Take each one in turn, and lay out the basic questions: what problem are we trying to solve? What alternatives to solving it are there? What are the tradeoffs in each alternative? By breaking it down and asking questions you expose more thinking to light, make it possible

for others to ask questions, and make it more difficult for
anyone to defend a bad idea.

No one can ever take away your right to think things over,
especially if the decision is important. If your mind works best
in 3rd or 4th gear, find ways to give yourself the time needed
to get there. If when you say "I need the afternoon to think
this over", they say "Tough. We're deciding now", ask whether
the decision is important. If they say yes, you should be
completely justified in asking for more time to think it over and
ask questions.

And yet more reasons

I'm sure you have stories of your own follies dealing with
smart people defending bad ideas, or when you, yourself, as a
smart person, have spent time arguing for things you regretted
later. Given the wondrous multitude of ways the universe has
granted humans to be smart and dumb at the same time, there
are many more reasons why smart people behave stupidly. For
fun here's a few more.

- Smart people can follow stupid leaders (seeking praise
  or promotion).

- Smart people may follow their anger into stupid places.

- They may be trained into stupidity.

- Smart people can inherit bad ideas from their parents
  under the guise of tradition.

- They may simply want something to be true, that can
  never be.

WHY YOU ARE NOT AN ARTIST

Picasso. van Gogh. Beethoven. Hendrix. Kurosawa. Kafka. Magritte. Bukowski. These are people most agree are worthy of the title "Artist." But what if you met them before they were famous?

In their own lives, certainly for van Gogh, or Kafka, they didn't have fame. And in the case of many Artists, including Magritte and Bukowski, their work wasn't widely accepted until late in their careers. We'd need some other criteria than success to identify them for what they are.

My argument is whatever criteria we'd invent, few of us would meet it. The artists mentioned had a dedication to their work, and a threshold for risk, well beyond ours.

And this isn't solely because of our (lack of) talent – instead my point is to be an Artist requires a specific intent. An intent that nearly everyone with a full time job does not have while doing that job. You might be an artist in your spare time, but that's something else entirely.

While you might have grand aesthetics in your work, or amazing skills that seem magical to others, that is mere artistry. How you employ those talents determines whether you are an Artist or not. And sure, you might be the best in your field at designing websites or selling cars, but that's mastery. The big question is this: your mastery of skill is used in service of what? A corporation? Some stockholders? Customer satisfaction? These might be honorable pursuits, perhaps noble in some sense, but that's not enough to call it art.

Think of *Guernica*, *The Seven Samurai*, *The Mona Lisa*, or your favorite work by your favorite Artist. What is it about their creations that influences you? It's more than just talent. It has something to do with the aims they used their talent for. We wouldn't put a box of laundry detergent (except perhaps for Warhol), or a piece of business software, however wonderfully designed they might be, in the same class of creative effort. We all know there is a distinction between one kind of thing and another.

I think to call someone an Artist means that they have a sense of higher purpose beyond commerce. Not that they don't profit from their work, or promote themselves, but that the work itself has spiritual, philosophical, emotional or experiential attributes as central goals. An Artist's work is about an idea, a feeling, or an exploration of a form, framed more by their own intuitions, than the checklists and protocols of bureaucracies and corporations.

Simply put, there are three main points:

1. An Artist is committed to their ideas in ways most people are not. An Artist will risk many things: wealth, convenience, popularity, fame or even friends and family to protect the integrity of their ideas. If you're not risking anything, and mostly doing what you are told, you're probably not an Artist.

2. This means anyone who constantly sacrifices their

own ideals, and regularly makes major compromises to satisfy the inferior opinions of "superiors" they do not respect, can not sincerely call their work Art. And therefore, can not call themselves Artists.

3. An Artist is willing to sign their name on what they give to the world. Are you proud of what your company makes? Does it go out the door with even half the soul you put into your designs? If you ship things to the world that are beneath your own bar, can you call it art in the same way you would if it met that bar?

The definition game rarely leads anywhere. You can find many different definitions for the words art, artist and artistry to support any point of view, as it's an active area of debate. But my favorite definition of an Artist is:

1. A person who creates, by virtue of imagination, talent or skill, works of aesthetic value, especially, but not limited to, the fine arts.

2. A person who creates art (even bad art) as an occupation.

If you make paintings, movies, novels or similar things, you're likely an Artist. Even if your work sucks (however we determine that), and even if you do it part time, or have never been paid a dime for your art, you still qualify.

But if you work for clients/bosses in the making of things that you yourself would not consider art, or are beneath your own standard, or that you blame others you work with for ruining, you are not an Artist. You are an employee. You are being paid to give someone else authority over your creative decisions. This can involve inspiration, effort, sacrifice, passion, brilliance, and many other noble things, but it's not the same as being an Artist.

HOW TO CONVINCE ANYONE OF ANYTHING

Most people do not like confrontation. The word argument itself tends to make people think of lawyers or divorce proceedings, or other unpleasant things. I prefer a more positive word: convince. The goal is to persuade, to make people want to agree with you and feel happy, or smart, or right, when they do. This has higher odds of success than bludgeoning them with logic, or trying to pin them into a mental submission hold. If you use your brain power to bend people's mind into a pretzel, it's likely once you turn away they'll squirm right back out to the shape they had before you got involved. And they'll likely resent you for twisting them up, too.

It's good to know our species sucks at convincing others and being convinced, or acting on those new ideas. Check out the stories of Moses, Jesus, Buddha, Muhammad, Socrates…some of our greatest minds, perhaps our greatest people, tried to convince their followers of some pretty simple ideas (e.g., do not kill, the Golden Rule), ideas which were often ignored or perverted by their followers in less than a generation. If this crowd couldn't pull it off with the name of God, the threat of damnation, or the gift of enlightenment behind them, the odds for the rest of us can't be good. If you have ideas or a mission, no matter how persuasive you are, most people will not hear you. Most people will not change. The bet is some will, and that's enough reward. And that your own thinking will sharpen through the process regardless of the outcome.

The secret behind all the skills of pitching, persuading, selling or inspiring is knowing the person you are talking to. There is no magic recipe for convincing large numbers of people of something all at the same time. That's really hard to do. But if you are only trying to convince one person of something, study their point of view and use that knowledge as a foothold for the ideas you want them to support.

If you are in a meeting with five other people, identify the most influential people in that room. Those are the people your pitch needs to be aimed at. The narrower your focus, the better your aim.

A classic mistake people make is focusing on their own pitch. Their points. Their slides. Entirely forgetting who the audience is. This is shooting blind. Instead, work the opposite way. Understand your audience's goals, beliefs and preferred kind of thinking (data driven, story driven, principle driven, goal driven) – how do they argue for things? How do they convince others to do things? That's the menu to work from. But most people find this boring. They can't excite their egos by studying other people, so they don't. And then they fail. But if you can be generous of mind, and, like a method actor, put yourself inside their view of the world, you will understand them. And once you understand them you'll see their perspective on you and your ideas.

I know if I can find a way to connect my idea to something

they themselves argue and fight for, my chances improve. And if I can't convince them, my study of how they think, combined with their refutation of my ideas, will teach me something new about their view of things. At a minimum, their counterargument will give me new knowledge that will help me the next time I have to convince them, or someone else, of something. Or it might convince me they are unconvincable, and my time is best spent elsewhere. Or most powerful and interesting of all, that what I'm arguing for isn't as good at I think it is.

I also know I have to believe in the idea myself and for the right reasons. If I'm not convinced it's hard to convey conviction. But if I can enter a conversation and honestly state "I believe so much in this idea I'd bet half this year's salary on it" or "If I'm wrong I'll do your chores this month," whoever is listening will feel an undeniable sincerity. Sometimes this can work as a bluff, but that's a bad habit to start. If you get good at this kind of deception, you'll find yourself persuading others to do things you barely understand, which serves no one.

ATTENTION AND SEX

What things in your life demand undivided attention? Whatever they are, they define your life more than anything else you do. Your obituary will not list the hours you fought off boring meetings or ignored your friends by reading forgettable blurbs about forgettable things on your cell phone or laptop. What matters are the intimate, deep moments that refuse division. The wise and happy throughout history have found ways to avoid situations that demand divided attention. They convert the fractured experience into the meaningful, and perhaps magical, by investing their attention wisely.

There isn't a single great work in the history of civilization— no novel, symphony, film, or song—that was completed as a one-fifth time-slice between web browsing, text messages and television. Despite the modern drive to consume things made by others, time will always be our most finite resource and it crumbles when split into tiny little pieces. It's up to us to choose how much of life is spent passively (consuming, waiting, watching) vs. actively (thinking, feeling, doing, making). Whatever we choose, when we die, we have no one to blame but ourselves for where our time, and attention, went.

Free money and sex if you read this now! (Laying the attention trap)

We're told our senses bring us the world, but the opposite is more accurate: our senses filter the world down to what we've needed to survive. Our eyes see only a fraction of the kinds of light around us (e.g., ultraviolet, infrared). We can only see 140 degrees of 360 meaning we see less than 50% of what is going on at any time around our bodies. The human range of hearing is comically bad compared to most house pets and insects. In short, our senses are designed to focus our attention on what matters for our survival. Our senses ignore many times more data than they bring to our brains. It's knowing what to ignore that makes us successful, not how many volumes of data we can consume at the same time. Successful athletes, performers, or writers about how they consistently perform at high levels and they'll tell you about focus, and the discipline of centering their attention on what they're doing. They practice and drill so that basic tasks become so familiar they don't have to think about them anymore, focusing instead on the details most of us miss.

The challenge is that in the last 50 years we've designed things purposefully to attract attention. TV commercials, websites, and advertisements of all kinds are machines that, by design, take advantage of our limited means of perception. We know that red, fast, sexy, blinking things play on our reptilian brains and few can resist granting attention to them. This is an old tactic, as flowers, fruits, and plants have played similar games for eons, just not on the same scale. No flower has ever spent millions researching strategies for advertisements, training a species over time to eat when it's not hungry, or to compulsively seek information for information's sake. Yet our manmade attractions do this every day. In a prehistoric age, creatures competed for survival. In an information age, we, as corporations and people, compete for each other's attention. We're supposed to be in a golden age of leisure time since most hard labor is done for us, but somehow we've fallen into a place where time gained from innovations falls away like sand between our hands, phones and keyboards.

The law of lost attention

The danger of misguided attention is this: how we spend our attention changes the value of what we spend it on. If you participate in potentially intimate activities, like sports, conversation, or non-casual sex (meaning both emotionally and physically intimate), treating them with split attention will inevitably make them non-intimate experiences. Like a flower that doesn't get enough water, an intimate experience can only grow to the depth and quality of the time given to it. If you only spend a fast food amount of attention, you will never have a five-star dining experience (consider the slow food movement.) The same applies to everything: relationships, talents, experiences. Fast food (and sex) can be fun, but it's unlikely to be fulfilling if that's all you have. They work best as counterpoints to deeper, slower, more wonderfully intimate things.

Law of lost attention: The value of something you spend attention on, is dependent on how much attention you spend on it.

Whenever someone is lost in waves of e-mail and information, they're often oblivious to the deepest tragedy of their time. It's not the stress of dealing with so many requests and obligations (as real and challenging as that stress might be). It's that somewhere in the wash of interactions and split attentions is the missed possibility they're looking for: meaning. Depth of experience. Connection. To quote Robert Pirsig, "The truth knocks on the door and we say, 'Go away. I'm looking for the truth.'" In the race to clean out inboxes and scratch items off the to-do list, we miss chances to find the thing we've created the inbox and to-do list for. Like an American tourist in Europe racing from site to site with barely a moment to take a picture or talk to someone not on their tour bus, we're trapped in a quantity mentality, despite our quality based desires.

Reclaiming attention

We are information insecure. The compulsion for more is driven by lack of confidence in what we already have. Out of a secret kind of fear we are convinced that the next e-mail or link is better than the one we're reading now. The result is a private rat race: what does it mean to stay on top of information that doesn't satisfy?

The unspoken dream is to be attention rich. To have enough attention that at any time we're comfortable digging in to something that we connect with. But if we're always spending our attention as though it has no value, and we're attention poor, we don't have enough attention to spend even when we find the things we're looking for.

It's true that the hunt and intensity of multitasking can be fun – there are thrills in chasing things, physical or virtual, but most evidence shows we perform worse when we multitask. Despite how it feels, it appears our minds don't work best when we split our attention. And given the law of lost attention, we may be multitasking over the very experiences we're multitasking to find.

Reclaiming attention starts with a leap of faith in believing the following sentence: you do not need more than what you have. When you survive that leap, which you will, it's easy to convince yourself that you need less of the attention consuming things in your life than you currently have. You'll soon find that every important ambition for your life is best served by treating your attention with the conservation it deserves. Instead of splitting your mind to keep busy, move your body to somewhere worthy of all the attention you have.

The attention challenge

Here's a test to help sort out how your attention is working for you. Make a list of all the things you read, check, skim, or browse every day (include your gadgets). Make a second list of why you're spending your attention on them. What are you trying to achieve or feel? Rank the first list based on the second. Then cut the first list in half or by one third and see what happens.

A STRAWMAN FOR EVERYTHING

We need to ask more questions. Information is cheap today but it's worthless without good questions to shape it into meaning. The news tells us about a murder in town, or the unemployment rate, or the fluffy cat saved in the tree, but what are we to do about this? Why is it how it is? Who decides these are the best things to tell us and why? From the cradle to the grave we are given information as if it were precious, but it's not anymore. We're overwhelmed by it. To paraphrase Neil Postman, information is a form of garbage and yet we're oddly addicted to cramming more of it in our brains. What's rare is wisdom for thinking about information, and that starts with asking questions about it. What is a fact? Why was this fact chosen instead of another? The skill of asking good questions is something we are never taught in school (schools being places we're mostly rewarded for giving the "right" answer). We need to cultivate question asking as a skill, recognize the distinctions between information, knowledge, and wisdom, and align our energy in relation to the relative importance of these three different things.

We confuse tech progress with social and personal progress. The 20th century was the most technologically advanced, yet also had the most bloodshed in history . This doesn't mean the former caused the latter, but it certainly didn't prevent it. More recently, the web, for all its wonders, did not prevent misleading information from leading the U.S. into war in Iraq. New technology guarantees almost nothing. Social progress, more freedom, less cruelty, personal enlightenment, lifetime fulfillment, and more, all depend less on technologies than self-awareness and will. The U.S. Constitution was written using quill pens. The Civil Rights Movement was fueled by marches and speeches. Buddha, Jesus, and Socrates did all their deeds without even the dream of electricity. The Internet, the iPad, or whatever comes next are unlikely to be the prime mover in social progress as history demonstrates technology is rarely the missing link: our self-awareness and commitment to change often are. Technology can certainly help, but the heavy lifting is always on us.

Integrity is the proximity of your beliefs to your actions, and we need more integrity. It's very easy to preach from the *Bible* about the good Samaritan, or about the freedoms of the U.S. Bill of Rights, but we forget these ideals when it's inconvenient. I wish there was some way to put an integrity score over people's heads, floating around for all to see, as there'd be less posturing and preaching from those who fail at precisely the things they criticize in others. I'm starting to judge people less by my own values, and more by how their actions match their own proclaimed values. Unlike the status symbols of cars and clothes, there is no easy status symbol for one's integrity. I don't know how I would score myself, but part of why I write is to keep tabs on my own score. Fulfillment in life depends on integrity, and integrity doesn't depend on money or gadgets. Considering Enron, Madoff, WMDs, and the sub-prime crisis, one story of this age is lost integrity. I wonder how to push things the other way.

There is a downward spiral of empty consumption. When George W. Bush, after 9/11, told us the best thing Americans can do is to buy, something bizarre happened to us. He had the greatest leadership moment of my lifetime in his hands – he could have told us anything at all, plant trees, volunteer in schools, send gifts to GIs, and like in WWI and WWII, the country, and some of the world, would have passionately rallied together to work for a shared cause. But he told us to "live our lives and hug our children" and to buy for ourselves: "I ask your continued participation and confidence in the American economy." I think we all knew there was something missing from this, but didn't know what it was. And as a nation, despite our many religions, one kind of faith Americans share is the faith in buying things.

Now, I like buying things. I like the computer I'm typing on, and I like the car I drive, but I don't have faith that a better computer or better car will make me happier than the ones I already have. Many people I know want more community, love, and meaning in their lives, yet spend their life energy working hard to earn more money to buy things they don't need, things that will never help them get more community, love or the meaning they seek. Advertising convinces us otherwise, and we like being convinced. We're terrified of our economy falling apart, an economy dependent on consumption. I don't know how we get out of this loop, but it seems to be a problem, and as Jared Diamond is fond of suggesting, this likely can't last very long.

This is the greatest time in history for creatives. When I talk to groups about creativity, few notice how it's cheaper and easier than ever to make creative work and get it out into the world. If born in our age, Thomas Paine, Picasso, Mozart or Voltaire would have loved to have been bloggers, or YouTube video makers, having instant access to the world for their ideas. da Vinci, Michelangelo, and van Gogh would have had websites, thrilled to get commissions via Kickstarter and PayPal from complete strangers, freeing them from working only at the frustrating whims of popes and kings. Making music, film, books or almost anything at all is cheaper than ever in history, and can be put out into the world without a single person's approval. We are free! The gatekeepers are gone! There are no external excuses anymore. The only reason you are not making the things you dream about , or support others who do what you wish you could do, is you, and how you think about you.

What is your strawman for everything?
Tell me at www.scottberkun.com/strawman

EPILOGUE

You've made it to the end. I'm happy you're here, but it's a bittersweet occasion. There are no more essays to read in this book. Pity that. If you want more, please visit: www.scottberkun.com.

Meanwhile, I can tell you about how this book was made.

For a time I planned for this book to have 15 new essays, but as the project progressed that goal fit less and less. Since the 30 essays here were written over the span of 10 years, it was hard to write new pieces that would make sense as an additional section. I drafted many essays and had a surplus of ideas, but decided they'd be better off published elsewhere, probably online. The book was simple and strong all on its own.

The title for the book was inspired by the writings of Emerson. He often referred to the creative mind as a fire and wrote about ways to ignite the mind. His essay *Self-Reliance* was a profound influence, and his life has been one inspiration for shaping my own.

I learned to write essays by reading them, and I offer this as advice to anyone who wishes to write. For years before I quit my regular job to write full time, I read Montaigne, Voltaire, Emerson and others, writers who invented and defined the form known as the essay. If they were alive today they'd be online, writing on the web, reveling in the commentary and interaction provided by the web's many freedoms. It's worth noting many things I write are inspired by comments and emails from readers online, and I'm grateful to them. This book would not exist without their energy and support. I always welcome ideas to write about or questions readers want me to answer.

I often read collections of essays, the kinds of books used to torture unsuspecting college English majors. A favorite is the annual collection called *Greatest American Essays*. It's refreshing to discover how many different ways good writers can use 2,000 words or less. Another favorite annual collection is the *Best American Nonrequired Reading*, edited by David Eggers. Books comprised of diverse essays aren't liked by everyone, but I love them. If I read an essay I don't like, I skip it and move on. It's a great way to discover writers new to me.

I've written close to 1,500 essays and articles, yet a mere 30 appear in this volume. The 30 were chosen to be readable by anyone, with any background and any interest. I wanted to make a book I could give to almost anyone and have it be interesting to them and get them thinking, and interested in what I'll write about next.

Thanks for reading this far, and I hope you'll read more.

-Scott info@scottberkun.com / www.scottberkun.com

HOW TO HELP THIS BOOK IN 60 SECONDS

Thank you for buying (cough cough, stealing, cough) this book. If it exceeded your expectations or left you thining, "Gee, things would be better if everyone read this", this page is for you, because I need your help.

I'm an independent author. This book was entirely self-published. I don't have a huge marketing machine behind me, nor a gang of billionaire friends, or even a magic genie offering wishes. But that's ok. If you're willing to give a minute, you can seriously help this book find its way in the cold, tough world, where many good books never reach all the people they should.

Please consider any of the following:

- Write a review on amazon.com. It's the simplest way to share your opinions of this book to others who are considering it.

- Post about this book to your blog, on Facebook or on Twitter

- Recommend the book to coworkers, your friends and your friends friends, or even your friends with blogs, or your coworkers friends who blog, or even your friends of friends who blog about their friends blogs. The possibilities are endless.

- If you know people who write for newspapers or magazines drop them a line, or perhaps Oprah or Jon Stewart owe you a favor. If so, now is a good time to cash it in.

- If you like to pretend you're a secret agent, sneak past the desk of someone important, and leave a copy of this book on their desk.

- Subscribe to the mailing list on www.scottberkun.com, or to the blog itself and automatically get the great things I write about each week.

These little things make a huge difference. As the author my opinion of the book carries surprisingly little weight. But you, dear reader, have all the power in the world.

As always, thanks for your help and support.

NOTES AND REFERENCES ON THE ESSAYS

If you've read my other books you know I take great care to reference other works. However given the history of these writings, and the fact they were written over many years, what follows is mostly notes and commentary. The thrill of writing the style of short essays found in this book is they're intellectual sprints. Like a conversation in a bar, over a few drinks, the value is the ideas and where they take you, rather than sources, origins or even support for claims. For this section I've gone through my notes and journals to offer some perspective not found in the essays themselves.

It was surprising to learn how many of these essays were written in 2010. It was only after vetting through several rounds of possibilities that the essays for this book were selected, and only when writing this section did I realize many of them were written around the same time.

1. The Cult of Busy (Published, March 12, 2010)

I've long been interested in understanding time. Robert Grudin's

Time and the Art of Living was an early read and paved the way for other temporal investigations. Bertrand Russell's essay "*In Praise of Idleness*" as well as Stephen Robins' *The importance of being idle* were definitely things I read at the time, or before, I wrote the *Cult of Busy*. Years later I read *A Geography of Time* by Robert V. Levine, which is also excellent and perspective changing. I read Csíkszentmihályi's work *Flow*, and flow states of perception of time in several forms, and saw him speak once here in Seattle. A major reason I quit my job in 2003 was to have more control over how I used my time.

2. Wants vs. Beliefs, (January 15, 2010)

It's hard to identify sources for this as I've read so many philosophy books over the last two decades. Formally these sorts of questions are epistemology, or asking how do we know what we know, or believe, which is a topic as old as philosophy itself. The Stoics, a group of Greek philosophers, were fond of behaving based on a realistic view of things despite what our desires would prefer. For me wants vs. beliefs is a perennial challenge, as logically we know the difference, but functionally our emotions influence our thinking more than we like to admit.

3. How to be a free thinker (January 6, 2009)

Bertrand Russell's essay *Why I am not Christian* (the lead essay in his book with the same name) demonstrated how someone could bravely ask questions despite the consequences. I didn't agree with everything in the book, but I cherished his passionate attempt to ask important questions about important things at a time before these questions were publically acceptable. Russell's career exemplifies free thinking in many ways, as he was never afraid of where the power of reason took him. Russell's career, like Emerson's, is a constant source of inspiration.

4. How to detect bullshit (August 9, 2006)

One of my earliest bosses, Eric Berman, told me, during a performance review, that I have a fantastic bullshit detector. I'd never thought of it before as an ability, but I realized then it's something rarely discussed in books or schools, but has great influence on a person's ability to be useful. Most of the tactics mentioned are things I learned first hand from debates at the family dinner table, or in the chaos of working with passionate people, people who make things. I did read Henry G. Frankfurt's popular book *On Bullshit*, but I found it disappointing. The one takeaway from that book was the idea that bullshitters are not aiming primarily to lie, but merely not to get in trouble.

The curious thing about this essay is the comments it received online were dominated by people questioning my interpretation of the *Bible*. I have no problem with interpretations that differ from mine, but I do have a problem when someone tells me in certain terms what a paragraph in a book means, when the paragraph itself doesn't offer much detail. I'm fond of putting myself inside narratives, whether they're the Bible or novels, and asking questions I would ask if I were there. That's the only way I can fully consider the challenges of a story, fictional or not. Questions like these are the kind a freethinker would ask.

5. Should you be Popular or Good? (April 9, 2009)

If you make things as part of a craft or art, you will eventually ask this question. We often label music bands that try too hard to be popular as sellouts. Why? Some artists wish to be great, which demands not primarily seeking popularity, but instead seeking to make great things. But once you're successful enough to survive at your craft, should something other than popularity drive your choices? I think yes. This book is an exploration of this very idea for my own career. This book is not a sequel to my other books, and I suspect it won't be as popular as they are.

6. There are two kinds of people: complexifiers and simplifiers (July 20, 2006)

I meet people at conferences or parties who are trying too hard to sound smart. I don't like spending time with these people. Talking to them is more about their egos than whatever they're pretending to talk about. My favorite people in the world are smart, but confident enough in their smarts not to have to prove it every minute by making things more complex than they need to be. There's a certain maturity required to see how much harder simplicity is to obtain than complexity. If you can speak simply about complex things I'll want to listen forever. Simplicity is a theme I've explored from many different dimensions. It's a common theme in design and architecture, found in books like Victor Papanek's *Design for The Real World*, and in the wisdom of philosophers like Saint-Exupéry who wrote "Perfection is attained, not when no more can be added, but when no more can be removed."

7. Are you indifferent? (April 23, 2010)

This was originally published with the title: *The Challenge of Indifference*. I miss those high-school days when it seemed easy to find people willing to be silly and make crazy things. Alan Watts' book *The Book: On The Taboo against knowing who you are* helped me rediscover the paradoxes of identity, and how much of my high-school age self I should never forget. Children are much better at being in the moment than adults and it's ironic that adults spend so much of their time wishing they felt the kinds of joy they did as children, yet resist stripping away all the layers they've constructed to protect themselves from that kind of joy. If nothing else, writing this essay makes me pay more attention whenever I see a street performer. Unlike panhandlers, they're offering their work in exchange for something. And for some of them, attention is an acceptable form of payment.

8. Does transparency matter? (August 26, 2010)

George Orwell wrote an essay called *"Politics and the English language"*, where he establishes the dangers of abusing words and phrases. I read it years ago, and it reaffirmed my suspicions. I've become sensitive to word abuse, especially jargon and buzzwords. Transparency as a popular junk word is on the decline, but it's still used enough to make questioning its use worthwhile.

9/10. How I found my passion / How to be passionate (May 13, 2010 / Jan 20, 2010)

I've always been opinionated. I think everyone is opinionated, but we use that word to mean people who more often express their opinions or do so with greater force. I think of passion as energy, and if you pick the right thing, we're all passionate. It's just a question of how courageous we are at letting it out, and developing the craft of expressing it in ways others appreciate. Henry Rollins' approach to his own life, as explored in his book *Get in the Van*, was hugely inspirational to me in my early 20s. His complete commitment to his goals and dreams made me rethink my commitments to how I was spending my own life. "Never do anything by half" is great advice.

11. On God and Integrity (Jan 12, 2010)

I read scripture because the roots of the tree are the only way to understand the branches and the leaves. Many great minds, like Newton and Jefferson, have questioned the practice of Christianity and other religions in their own times and I've was influenced by their bravery. To make God and faith about yourself violates the principles of every religion I've ever studied, yet it's common practice that goes uncriticized.

12. Hating vs. Loving (August 31, 2009)

On a road trip with Chris McGee from Seattle to Bannff in the winter of 2000, I stayed at a youth hostel. After too much whiskey, I asked a young man from Greece what book, after drinking with me for many hours, he thought I most needed to read. The book was *Living, Loving and Learning*, by Leo F. Buscaglia.

13. The surprise inspiration of death (May 20, 2010)

I think this life is all we get. I might be wrong, but like the Stoics, I'll assume I'm right on this one until proven otherwise. I have several whiteboards in my office, and one of them contains a list of aphorisms that help me focus. Near the top is "You could be dead." If ever I feel lazy or unmotivated, thinking hard about the fact today could be my last day, surfaces a surprising amount of energy.

14. How to make a difference (December 13, 2005)

There is an American archetype , seen in after school specials and Hollywood films, that the goal of life is to make a difference. Typically it's grand things that qualify, but reading books about Eastern philosophy has convinced me otherwise. It's small things, done consistently, that can matter just as much or more, depending on where you stand. One of my favorites is *Chop Wood, Carry Water*, by Taylor, Weyler and Ingrasci. I read it in a freshman philosophy course at Drew University, and it's a general primer on mindfulness. Another is *Crazy Wisdom*, By Wes Nisker.

15. Why you must lead or follow (May 18, 2005)

I have this growing sense as I age that most people spend most of their lives standing in the dead limbo between leading and following. They complain about those who lead with sufficient conviction that they will never follow them, but yet they don't have the courage or confidence to lead themselves. So they sit and wait as life passes by. When I feel stuck or disappointed or a thousand other things, I ask myself "lead or follow." The best use of my time is spent either leading something or following something good done by someone else. As lazy as I can be, I'm more prone to leading than following, but if I'm too scared to lead, I should at least find someone to follow.

16. Why the world is a mess: a theory (May 13, 2010)

The secret entertainment of an essay like this is how many essays throughout history sound exactly the same. Socrates, Lao Tzu, Jefferson, Voltaire and Shakespeare all complained about the folly of man. It's great fun to take big swings like this, even knowing I can't possibly connect fully - I know it's not as simple as I suggest, because of how many people in the past have made the same observations, and how little impact they had on the general trends.

17. The size of ideas (October 1, 2010)

I wrote this article for Harvard Business Review in October, 2010. It was a response to going to too many conferences, where too many consultants made too many empty claims about their grand theories of innovation. Small things do matter if you know what to do with them. Subtlety and nuance can be more powerful than raw force.

18. Book Smarts vs. Street Smarts (February 9, 2010)

A reader of scottberkun.com suggested this topic. I like to think of myself as someone who has some of both, but I suspect most people do. One of the notions hinted at here is the idea of public vs. private school. I went to public school in NYC and I have no complaints. There were enough opportunities for me to pursue book smarts, and plenty of situations forced upon me that taught street smarts. The isolating effects of suburbia, and private schooling, makes it harder to learn some of the things young adults need to know.

19. Why does faith matter? (July 29, 2010)

It's tricky to write about this topic. This was an essay I reviewed and revised dozens of times. I was trying to avoid falling into the obvious pitfalls most religious debate ends up in. I wrote another essay called "Innovation vs. Tradition: Christianity, the Vatican and Sin" which asks similar questions, but more provocatively. If you want a more forceful take on similar turf, you can find this essay on scottberkun.com.

20. Can you be great, with grace? (July 22, 2010)

My friend Royal Winchester and I debated this over drinks. Many blog posts and essays are born from conversations I have with people on email, in comments on the blog and even in real life! Amazing. One of my favorite things to do is discuss big ideas with friends over great food, drink and fire. I'd like to arrive at a formula for greatness, or for evaluating greatness, and apply it to the names typically mentioned as living great lives. It would be interesting to see how they scored given the variable of people who knew them closely. I'd also like a roadmap to try and follow.

21. How to give and receive criticism (September, 2004)

Some of this I learned from my wife, who, as an art major in college, regularly experienced critiques of her work by her peers. It's sad how few other disciplines see giving and receiving feedback important enough to make it part of their curriculum. These two abilities are another unspoken set of skills that helps explain why some people are more productive collaborators.

22. How to learn from your mistakes (July 17, 2005)

For the years I worked as a team leader I've been fascinated by failure. First was Petroski's To Engineer Is Human, which spawned an interest that led to dozens of different books on failure in different fields. All projects are made of people and eventually my attitudes about learning from failure at work became my attitudes about learning from failure in anything. In many ways being able to learn at all depends on being willing to learn from mistakes.

23. How to keep your mouth shut (September 18, 2009)

I used to think the loudest, smartest person in the room had the most power. But the person who doesn't need to say much to make what they want happen is certainly smarter, and likely more powerful. "You have to pick your battles" is simple advice some people never learn.

24/25. Creative thinking hacks / Dr. Seuss and wicked constraints (August 7, 2007, January 8, 2009)

While researching *The Myths of Innovation* I read dozens of books on creativity and the history of ideas. I taught a course at the University of Washington, and that experienced reinforced my belief that creativity is simple. If you get yourself to make things and follow a handful of rules, it happens all on its own. This list of hacks was the backbone of the course. The Dr.Seuss story was one that surfaced during research but didn't fit anywhere. It eventually surfaced on the blog, and now here.

26. Why smart people defend bad ideas (April, 2005)

This was written years before I'd learn about Cognitive Bias. If you want to spend a fun afternoon learning specific traps even smart people can fall into, do a few web searches on that term. I'd love to write a book exploring this theme and how many smart people have failed because of these biases.

27. Why you are not an artist (June 15th, 2010)

The secret that's not in this essay is I'd like to be an artist. I'd like to make art. And although I do make things that are creative and have a certain style, I wouldn't call myself an artist for the reasons offered in this essay. I get cranky when people misappropriate the word.

28. How to convince anyone of anything (March 10th, 2010)

Research for my third book, *Confessions of a Public Speaker*, included studying rhetoric. The art of persuasion and logical argument is ancient, and was a preoccupation of the Greeks. This essay was simply a conversational distillation of the most basic idea of what persuasion is. Watch a charming young man try to convince a pretty young girl to go on a date, and you'll see many of the same ideas. Persuasion is everywhere if you look for it.

29. Attention and Sex (March 21, 2006)

At Ignite! Seattle 2006, an event comprised of short presentations, I did a talk based on the ideas here. The essay was written around the same time, but published after the presentation. To this day I do try to spend as much time as I can doing thing and to socialize with people who are also willing to intimately share experiences. Phones have crept into all the corners of quiet time in our lives, and as fun to use as they can be, there is a price. Giving someone your full attention is increasingly rare and sacred.

30. A strawman for everything (April 8, 2010)

This was the 1,000th post on www.scottberkun.com. I stepped back to see if I could offer a summation of what I write about in a single short piece. I read many biographies and collected works and often they're about people who are dead. These books often have some pretentious introduction written by someone else telling you what the collective work of the person in question means. Since I'm not dead yet, I thought I'd offer a summary all by myself.

One pleasure of writing regularly is the opportunity to look backwards and make shapes from the pieces. It helps me think about what I want the next 1,000 writings to be about, and what I hope to be able to say about them when I look back after they're done.

ACKNOWLEDGMENTS

Only one name goes on the cover, but many people work hard to make a book. And it is always more people than you'd think.

Thanks to designer Tim Kordik and editor Krista Stevens for taking on this unusual project, which was stalled painfully long, on frustrating intervals, due to my indulgences. They worked to define what the book is and helped bring it together. Special thanks to Tim for his dedication, creative energy and most potently, his open mind. He was a joyous, hard working collaborator on what has been a most interesting journey - he'd be a treasure for any client.

Thanks to all the readers of www.scottberkun.com who contributed to choosing the title, cover design and dozens of other decisions. I read every comment you post and every email you send. Your support over the last decade has made the work found in this book possible. I want you to know I'm passionate about my future as a writer, and filling that bookshelf, in part because you remind me someone other than me reads what I write. I'm forever grateful for you for being, and helping grow, my audience.

For advice on self-publishing: Phil Simon, who patiently answered a thousand questions, and Joel Grus.

People who gave advice on the book, the outline and feedback on essays: Krista Stevens, Tim Kordik, Kimm Viebrock, Tiff Fehr, Andrea Winchester, Royal Winchester, Terrel Lefferts, Rob Lefferts, Jill Stutzman, Kav Latiolais, Richard Grudman, Neil Enns, Shawn Murphy, and Chris Hare.

To my amazing squad of copyeditors and proofreaders: Kav Latiolais, Tisha White, Susan Chopra, Chris Granger, Vasu Srinivasan, Piotr Tyburski, Branimir Corluka, Del Cooke, and Sara Vermeylen. You folks are the embodyment of tough love.

Kudos to my good friend, and escalope, Marlowe Shaeffer, the only person on earth who has worked with me on every single book, and lived to tell the tale. Like a caped crusader she appeared out of the darkness in the 11th hour to help edit and proofread the book (a heroic deed which may earn her a role in a future colophon).

For all my awesome supporters on kickstarter: Phil Simon, Dhruv Sood, Devin Reams, Yousef Omar, Jay Turpin, Jeremiah Andrick, Charles Pharis, Charles Miller, Chris Kenst, Michael Malcangio, Paolo Malabuyo, Dann Bergman, Dan Vogel, Robert Fayle, mpecher, Rachel, Tiff Fehr, Michael Sepcot, Dmitri Schoeman, Keith McCleary, João Adolfo Lutz, Kitt Hodsden, Ricardo Duarte, Laurel Swayze, Tero Parviainen, Luca Sartoni, JJ Casas, Jack Dempsey, Alessandra Farabegoli, Dirk Haun, Roberto Archila, Marek Prokop, Stefan Steinbauer, Steve Taylor, Sara Rosso, John Kearsing, Shan, Rob Staenke, John Daughtry, Lutz Seifert, Todor Vlaev, Paul Jensen, Chris Winters, Piotr Tyburski, Paul Tevis, Jim Harris, Tim Rodriguez, Christine Walker, Matt Dukes, Marc Majcher, Karen White, Josh Rensch, Richard S. Childers, Unmesh Gundecha, Mavis Turner, Jason Copenhaver, Bryce Johnson, Jens Johnson, Matthew Guay, Mike Erickson, Anders Olme, Chris Moule, Sree Harsha Kamireddy,

Christof Dorner, Deepak Surti, Donald Cox, Michael Nitabach, Dave Sollers, Bill Marty, Noel, Pamella Marschall, Sai Ganesh, Michelle Peterson, Waldo, Carl Rigney, Naveen Sinha, Mike Pearce, Hans Michael Krause, pornlover, Kirk Jackson, Petr Novak, Fabrizio, Gorielo, Shrix, Kesha, Marc van Agteren, Matthew Talbert, Travis Scott Collier, sperzdechly, Santiago Paiva, Gerald Choi, Danile Fritzler, Waldo's brother, Sebastian Tecsi, Aly Valli, Sajid Fakir, Brandy, Eric Nehrlich, Kevin Hale, Neil Enns, David Golden, Grace Kwon, Minh Nguyen, Charlie Compton, DJ Bauch, Xero Limited, Daryn Nakhuda, Hideo Aoki, Shawn Murphy, Vivek Gupta, Devin Hales, Anthony Kennedy, Ron Kersic, Rob Donoghue, Aaron Suggs, Pablo López-García, Raviapte, Ryan Ogborn, Mswaine, Volkan Unsal, Dilys Bohncke, Marcelo Neves, Ozan Yigit, David Farber, Alan Sweeney, Matthew Arcuri, Tomasz Matlak, Rod Dunican, swoicik, Waldo's evil twin, Greg Brake, Mark Meeker, Dan Saffer, Malcolm McKinnon, Tom Brands, Francois Roosegaarde Bisschop, rwalling, Patrick Vlaskovits, The guy who killed Waldo's evil twin and got away with it, Stephen Kellett, Haider and Pat Wehner.

To everyone who didn't answer my email: you could be here.

Thanks to Matt Mullenweg, and everyone who works on WordPress and at Automattic, Inc, especially Team Social (Mike Adams, Beau Lebens, Andy Peatling (former), Hugo Baeta, Tim Moore, Justin Shreve and John James Jacoby). I love you guys, but you're part of why this book took forever to publish. Stop being so cool - I'd write more.

To the Donner party: we almost fucked it up. Lets not do that again, ok? Glad we learned how to repair things, since it makes us stronger now than ever. By the way, the song playing right now is "Me and Julio Down By The SchoolYard" by Paul Simon. Score Scott 1, Donners 0.

Music listened to while working on this book: Cat Powers, The Cave Singers, The Decemberists, Aimee Mann, Man Man,

Tift Merrit, Mahler, Bruce Springsteen, The Civil Wars, Caspar Babypants (Run baby run, run run run run run), Elliot Smith, The Breeders, Ottorino Respighi, Patty Griffin, Ida Maria, The Kills, The Thermals, The Head and The Heart, Elizabeth and the Catapult, OK Sweetheart, Social Distortion, U2, and Tom Waits.

INDEX

I

ignorance   18, 26, 53, 77
inboxes   151
infinite number   94, 135, 137
information   40, 110, 112, 134, 150-2, 155-6
ingredients   120
inhibitions   122-3
innovation   15, 120-1, 151, 171-3, 193
integrity   53-5, 142, 156, 169
intelligence   135
intent   94-5, 97, 141
Inviting Disaster   109

J

Jefferson, Thomas   85, 169, 171
journal   44, 125, 165
joy   43, 168
judgment   58, 81, 96, 104, 125

K

Kafka   59, 141
kicker   53
kicker work   53
kicks   53-4, 60, 124
knowledge   24, 81-2, 94, 146-7, 155

L

laughter   111, 122, 126
lazy   12, 108, 124, 170
leaders   40, 58, 69-72, 86, 134, 139
leadership   70-2, 116
leap   152
learning   18, 47, 57, 103-7, 112, 129, 170, 172-3
lectures   47-8, 65, 117, 124, 193
legends   119-20
lessons   35, 39, 103, 106-7, 109-10, 138
level   48, 97, 135, 192
  wrong   135
leverage   78
life   12, 15, 19-20, 29, 36-7, 43, 45, 47, 54-5, 57-61, 64, 69, 149, 152, 169-70
  daily   15, 86
life energy   157
lifetime   45, 88, 157
listening   36, 75-6, 147
logic   26, 54, 77, 131-2, 138, 145
  tricks of   132-3
lost attention, law of   151-2
love   15, 57-8, 69, 95, 157, 162, 173, 178-9, 192
loving   54, 57, 169-70
lunches   76, 78, 105

M

Magritte   141
market economies, free   136-7
marketers   41
marketing   41
mastery   14, 142
McDonalds   78
Michelangelo   30, 124, 157
mistakes   54, 103-13, 172-3
  categorize   105
  complex   108, 111
  interesting   104, 106
  involved   106-7
  making   112
  person's   105
mistakes checklist   112
mode   126
moments   24, 53, 60, 107, 110, 149
money   66, 135, 156-7
mouth   19, 115, 117, 173
Mozart   119, 124, 157
multitasking   152
musicians   36, 48, 67, 121

N

names   21, 40, 87-8, 122, 124, 143, 166, 172, 177
nations   54, 83-4, 87, 157
network server   28
N.Y. Giants   53-4

O

objective measures   93-4
oil workers   109
online   7, 9, 161-2, 167
opinion   26-7, 34, 164
overhead projectors   39
owners   77, 117

P

Paine, Thomas   85, 157
paradox   187
parents   12, 18, 25, 40, 45, 83-4, 119, 122, 132, 137-9
parties   105, 131, 168
partners   87-8, 100, 127
passion   37, 43-4, 47-8, 143, 169
passionate   36, 43, 45, 47-8, 166, 169, 177
peers   43, 65, 72, 100, 124, 172
persistence   124, 130
personal preferences   97
perspectives   20, 93, 95, 101, 108, 111, 113, 122, 127, 146, 165-6
  good   95
persuading   71, 146-7, 174
Picasso   141, 157
piles   34, 45, 70, 106, 137
pitch   146
planet   66, 136
pool   95, 134, 138
popularity   29-30, 142, 167
possession   54, 94-5

power   34, 41, 71, 77, 105, 116-17, 133, 138, 164, 166, 173
praise   65, 67, 96, 116, 139
prayer   53-4
predictions   122, 137
prejudices   20
probe   26-7
problem   29, 40, 54, 64, 72, 77, 83, 95-8, 100, 105, 109, 124-6, 130, 135-8, 167
progress   19, 26, 64, 66, 70, 84-5, 103, 112, 116, 122
  social   156
project management   30
projects   26, 28, 48, 71, 98-9, 124, 127, 135, 161, 172, 177
psychology   23, 111, 132-3
publisher   8

Q

quality   12, 40, 64, 116, 133-4, 151-2

R

relax   14
religions   17, 19, 54, 83, 85-6, 157, 169
responsibility   72, 112
result   29-30, 113, 122, 137, 152
rewards   33, 41, 67, 100, 119, 146
risk   81, 84, 104, 141-2
role   72, 178
room   39, 49, 112, 116, 133, 146, 173
rules   17, 19, 82, 115, 117, 122, 138, 173
Russell, Bertrand   166

S

sacred texts   76
sacrifices   88, 142-3
Sally   39-40
sans-homework   25
schools   17-18, 25, 103, 119, 155, 157,

COLOPHON

This colophon will take a classic, Bauhausian approach to describing the diverse design elements used within and throughout this book. Unlike inferior colophons, and their makers (you know who you are), which don't explain their colophonic approach and presume the average reader's ability to make these distinctions on their own, this colophon will provide DVD style commentary throughout the colophon. First, we must introduce the many degrees of superiority this colophon has, or will have, compared to most you have seen and why you should be proud, even honored, to be reading this right now.

The colophon plan, one of many considered , and several prototyped and tested in three series of test trials performed in conjunction with the IOCA Platinum sub-committee on preliminary colophon research and investigation (PCRI), is to stick to the facts, providing the pure experience of exhaustive detail and esoterica we all dream about on long nights, when its too cold and wet outside, and we're too sad and lonely and beaten down by the indifferent winds of the world, too ashamed and filled with self-doubt to reach out to the ones we think, we hope, love us, knowing deep in our bones what we find at the end of our reach might be the only thing more terrifying than our fears – a moment of grace in our lives when we finally, at long last, after all the charades and dead ends, become whole.

May this humble little colophon, made from scratch using all-natural free-range locally raised text characters that were sent to private school and tutored personally only by individuals who won multiple Nobel and Pulitizer Prizes, characters cultivated, harvested and then imbued with the spirit of a 7th generation colophonist who was long retired but came very far out of retirement, just once, on an imbuing only exclusive contract, for this book. Long live the colophon(ist).

Cover fonts: Franklin Gothic Standard Extra Condensed and Trade Gothic Bold Condensed #20 (Yay! Bold!)

Numbers in section icons (gas can, sparks, fire): Trade Gothic Bold Condensed #20 (Look at the level of DETAIL. Amazing. I bet you didn't know you could get Trade Gothic condensed. Do you know how hard it is to condense a font? Ever done it? I don't think so. Fred Cheblanski once tried to condense Helvetica all by himself, got distracted just for a moment and spent the rest of the year in the hospital. To this day he can't even look at Helvetica. Although, who can).

Headlines: Franklin Gothic Standard Extra Condensed

Body Copy: Caecilia LT Std Light. (The font might look familiar because it's the same font used on Amazon Kindle devices. Isn't that clever of the author and designer? To pick the same font? Brilliant.)

Cover image: a profile of the author taken by Tim Kordik.

ABOUT THE AUTHOR

Scott Berkun is the best selling author of *The Myths of Innovation*, *Making Things Happen* and *Confessions of a Public Speaker*. His work as a writer and public speaker for hire have appeared in the *Washington Post*, *New York Times*, *The Economist*, *Wired Magazine*, *Fast Company*, *Forbes Magazine* and other media. He has taught creative thinking at the University of Washington and has been a regular commentator on CNBC, MSNBC and National Public Radio. His popular essays and entertaining lectures are free at www.scottberkun.com, where you can sign up for a monthly email of all his recent and best work. He tweets at @berkun.

THIS SPACE
FOR RENT

But it's very expensive so I don't recommend it, especially in this economy when interest rates are so low, you should just buy instead of renting.